THE BRISTOL OLD VIC

The first ten years

THE
BRISTOL
OLD VIC

The first ten years

BY

Audrey Williamson
& Charles Landstone

J. GARNET MILLER LIMITED

LONDON

MADE AND PRINTED IN GREAT BRITAIN BY
THE GARDEN CITY PRESS LIMITED
LETCHWORTH, HERTFORDSHIRE

Contents

Illustrations

The Theatre Royal, Bristol.   *Frontispiece*

BETWEEN PAGES 40 AND 41

The Directors: Hugh Hunt (1946-1949); Allan Davis (1950); Denis Carey (1950-1954); John Moody (1954-1957).

The Beaux' Stratagem (Farquhar), 1946. Pamela Brown, Faith Brook, Noël Willman, William Devlin, Kenneth Connor, Nora Nicholson. Setting and costumes by Tanya Moiseiwitsch.

Macbeth, 1946. Pamela Brown as Lady Macbeth.

An Inspector Calls (J. B. Priestley), 1946. Rosalie Crutchley as Sheila Birling and William Devlin as Inspector Goole.

BETWEEN PAGES 56 AND 57

The Playboy of the Western World (Synge), 1946. Cyril Cusack as Christy Mahon and Wendy Hiller as Pegeen Mike.

Much Ado About Nothing, 1947. Rosalie Crutchley as Beatrice and Clement McCallin as Benedick.

Much Ado About Nothing, 1947. Church scene. Modern dress production by Hugh Hunt. Rosalie Crutchley (Beatrice), Meriel Moore, Hilda Shroder (Hero), Clement McCallin (Benedick), Bettine Milne, Marne Maitland, Norman Claridge and Edward Stanley (Friar Francis).

Much Ado About Nothing, 1954. Church scene. Production by John Moody. Edward Hardwicke (Friar Francis), Edgar Wreford (Benedick), Perlita Neilson (Hero) and Rosemary Harris (Beatrice).

King Lear, 1947. William Devlin as Lear and Leon Quartermaine as Kent.

ILLUSTRATIONS

The Traveller Without Luggage (Anouilh), 1951. Laurence Payne as Gaston and Sheila Burrell as Juliette.

Love's Labour's Lost, 1951. Production by Hugh Hunt. Settings and costumes by Hutchinson-Scott.

Of Mice and Men (John Steinbeck), 1951. Setting by Patrick Robertson with Laurence Payne (George) and Michael Aldridge (Lennie).

The Love of Four Colonels (Peter Ustinov), 1952. George Hagan (Frappot), Arthur Howard (Rinder-Sparrow), Newton Blick (Breitenspiegel) and Michael Aldridge (Ikonenko).

The Wild Duck (Ibsen), 1953. Dorothy Reynolds (Gina), Maureen Quinney (Hedvig), Robert Eddison (Hjalmar Ekdal), John Neville (Gregers Werle).

Love for Love (Congreve), 1953. Maxine Audley (Mrs. Foresight), Robert Cartland (Scandal), Lee Montague (Ben), Dorothy Reynolds (Mrs. Frail).

BETWEEN PAGES 120 AND 121

Antony and Cleopatra, 1953. Yvonne Coulette as Cleopatra with Carol Marsh as Iras and Jeannette Sterke as Charmian.

Murder in the Cathedral (T. S. Eliot), 1954. Eric Porter as Becket and Basil Henson as the Fourth Tempter.

Marching Song (John Whiting), 1954. Edgar Wreford as General Forster and Ronald Hines as Captain Bruno Hurst.

The Merchant of Venice, 1955. Edgar Wreford as Shylock and Michael Allinson as Antonio.

No Sign of the Dove (Peter Ustinov), 1954. Paul Lee as Matthew and Perlita Neilson as Hope.

The Two Bouquets (Eleanor and Herbert Farjeon), 1954. Catherine Hutchinson (Kate Gill), Edgar Wreford (Edward Gill), Paul Lee (Mr. Gill) and Phyllida Law (Laura Rivers).

Salad Days (Reynolds–Slade), 1954. John Warner (Timothy), Eric Porter (Uncle Zed), Norman Rossington (Electrode), Eleanor Drew (Jane) and Bob Harris (Troppo).

ILLUSTRATIONS

Acknowledgements

THE AUTHORS WISH to thank Mr. Desmond Tripp for use of his large and valuable collection of photographs and also Mr. John Vickers, Mr. Kenny Parker and other photographers for their fine contribution; Miss Jane Wenham, Miss Rosalie Crutchley, Mr. Paul Lee, Miss Maureen Quinney, Mr. Denis Carey, Mr. Allan Davis and Mr. John Moody for the loan of photographs; Mrs. Margaret King and Mr. John Cairney for loan of Press cuttings; and Mr. John Moody, Miss Barbara Fox and the Bristol Old Vic management for allowing access to Press cuttings, programmes and play scripts.

Acknowledgement is also due to several Bristol critics—notably Mr. John Coe, Mr. Dennis Bushell, Mr. John Bennett, Mr. John Garrett and Mr. Peter Rodford—whose work for the three Bristol newspapers, the *Western Daily Press, Evening Post* and *Evening World*, has helped to provide a vivid historical record of plays and productions over the ten years covered.

CHAPTER ONE

The Theatre Royal
1766 *to* 1946

NEARLY EVERY BUILDING in Bristol's King Street is scheduled under the Act as an ancient monument. The centuries are spanned from the Tudor gables to the Georgian mansions which once housed the wealthy Bristol merchants. The oldest building is the dark timbered inn, the Llandowger Trow, the origin of whose name is lost in antiquity, but within whose precincts the Squire recruited Long John Silver and the rest of the pirate crew who were to sail with him to Treasure Island. Some of the buildings stand in shameful neglect and decay. The seventeenth-century almshouses at the corner of Charlotte Street form one long pitiful bomb-shattered shell. The peeling frontage of the Palladian Coopers' Hall disguises the fact that the interior, including the banqueting hall, with its painted ceiling, is used for storage by a wholesale fruiterer. Almost alone among the monuments, the Theatre Royal, built in 1766, stands alive and vibrant, renovated and decorative, still fulfilling the original purpose for which it was built.

It is the oldest theatre in the country. When it was built, King Street, adjacent to the docks, was the centre of the city's life and commerce. The merchants lived in their handsome houses on the other side of the road, or in the neighbouring Queen's Square, named after Queen Anne, and boasting a long terraced line of delicate ironwork balconies, in the style of architecture associated with the reign of that monarch. Always the theatre has had to struggle in an atmosphere of storm or stress, and, at the very outset, the idea of a permanent home of drama encountered the fierce opposition of the religious element in the city. Eighteenth-century Bristol had waxed rich on the slave trade, and when public conscience was aroused it found its expression in an excess of puritanism. There had been for the previous forty years a small theatre in what was then the countryside, half a mile outside the town, at the foot of Brandon Hill.

Run by an actor called Powel, who had been a leading man with Garrick at Drury Lane, this building had become too small for the growing theatrical interest of the town. (Chatterton speaks of this theatre as the 'hut at Jacob's Well'.) A plot of land was acquired in King Street and, despite the vehement local protests, a company of citizens was formed to promote the scheme. Chief among the organisers were Alexander Organ, who was subsequently to become mayor of the town, and Thomas Symons, a solicitor. They gathered around them forty-eight people, who each subscribed the sum of £50. In return these donors each received a silver token which gave them the right to a seat at one performance of every play produced in the theatre. Several of these tickets are still in existence, some of them at the Bristol Museum and Art Gallery. At least one was jestingly produced by its proud owner at the reopening of the theatre by C.E.M.A. in 1943. He waived his right to a seat.

Other money was subscribed, and the theatre eventually cost £5,000 to build. The foundation stone was laid on November 30th, 1764, and it was opened on May 30th, 1766. It had been built as a faithful replica of the Drury Lane Theatre of the day; James Paty was the architect and Michael Edkins the decorator. Very little of Edkins's craftsmanship remains today, but Paty's work is almost unaltered. There is still the sunken pit (now converted into stalls), the surrounding horseshoe circles which originally consisted of boxes, the entrances to which can still be seen in the woodwork at their rear. The gallery was added towards the end of the eighteenth century, and the highly decorative ceiling raised to meet it. The original entrance was down a long alleyway between shops and houses, and the theatre began at what is now the horseshoe foyer surrounding the dress circle. The conversion of this alleyway into a long entrance passage and the building of bars and offices above the passage are all Victorian additions. When a violent controversy (which reached the national Press) arose in 1955 about the pattern of the wallpaper in the entrance passage, the Ministry of Works, as guardians of an 'ancient monument', were careful to point out that they were not concerned, as their jurisdiction began only at the horseshoe foyer.

The theatre opened under the direction of Powel and two of his colleagues from Jacob's Well. The play was Steele's *Conscious Lover*, with a prologue that had been specially written by Garrick.

The latter, presumably in view of his old friendship with Powel, was present in the audience, and described the building as 'the most beautiful theatre in Europe'. Despite the interest that he showed on this occasion, Garrick himself never played at the theatre; his is, therefore, practically the only classic name in one hundred and ninety years missing from the list of actors and actresses who have trod the boards of King Street. The roll call includes, among many others, the Kembles, Sarah Siddons, Kean, Macready, Phelps, Irving, Forbes-Robertson, Ellen Terry, Tree and Sybil Thorndike.

The Puritans had not been able to prevent the building of the theatre. They were able to prevent the granting of a licence, however. To evade the law, the first performance was billed as 'A Concert of Musick and a specimen of Rhetorick'. It was given as a charity performance for the Infirmary, and £63 profit was afterwards handed over to that institution. Various other subterfuges were adopted for a number of years, and it was not until the theatre had been in existence for eleven years that a Royal Patent legalising the position was granted in 1777. The building which had previously been known as 'The Theatre' now and henceforth became the Theatre Royal.

The opening years of the theatre coincided with a great period of English drama. Goldsmith and Sheridan were at the height of their fame, and *She Stoops to Conquer*, *The School for Scandal* and *The Rivals* were all written in the 1770s. Each of these plays was produced at the Theatre Royal within a year or so of its production at Drury Lane and Covent Garden. In 1777, the year the Royal Patent was granted, the management of the theatre under John Palmer, junior, was amalgamated with that of Bath, whose theatre dated back to 1750, and was therefore older than that of Bristol. The original Bath Theatre was, however, destroyed by fire in the middle of the nineteenth century, and the present theatre was built in 1862.

Palmer inaugurated the system of interchange between stock companies in the two theatres, and, with occasional lapses, this plan was to continue for nearly a hundred years. It was a most fruitful period in the development of the English actor, and, in reality, the whole of the present-day repertory scheme, and the interchange between theatres, which is so strongly urged and fostered by the Arts Council, is simply a return to that system.

Sarah Siddons, smarting under the blow of her youthful failure at Drury Lane, joined John Palmer's company at a salary of £3 a week in 1778, and remained with him for four years before she returned in triumph to London. Three days of every week she played at the Theatre Royal in Bristol, and her dressing-room is still to be seen on the o.p. side of the stage. Various members of the Bristol Old Vic Company have claimed to have seen her ghost, but as she spent a very happy time in Bristol it is a kindly ghost and only appears to the believing.

In the early years of the nineteenth century the fortunes of the theatre began to decline. The character of Bristol had begun to change. King Street was no longer the centre of fashion. The spreading town had long since enveloped Brandon Hill, and was creeping out to the village of Clifton. In 1817 the forty-year-old connection with Bath was broken, and the Theatre Royal was on the market. In 1819 William Macready, father of the great William Charles Macready, became the lessee of the theatre. He issued an appeal to the public to support him and save the building from 'conversion into an arena for the display of Pugilistic Contests, and low mummeries, by which it must eventually be disgraced and polluted'. William Charles came down from Covent Garden to help his father launch the new venture. He appeared for three nights as Othello and then returned to London, although, until his retirement in 1851, he played many times at the Theatre Royal. The theatre was to remain in the hands of the Macready family for sixty-two years, and under them to enjoy the longest single stretch of prosperity in its history.

The elder Macready had led the harum-scarum life of a theatrical adventurer, but in his last ten years at Bristol he was happy and successful. He died in 1829 and was buried respectably in Bristol Cathedral. For the next four years William Charles held the lease on behalf of his stepmother, Catherine Desmond, who had been the elder Macready's leading lady, and had married him in 1821. In 1833 Mrs. Macready took over and continued in charge until her death in 1853. The connection with Bath had been taken up again after the death of the elder Macready, and, after another short break in the 1830s, it continued once more from 1845 to 1868. In the meantime the succession of the theatre had fallen to James Henry Chute, who had married the sister of William Charles Macready.

In all the years of the Macready family management, the stock company was among the best in the country. It was not, of course, very productive of good drama—in the whole literature of the English theatre from Sheridan's work in the 1770s to Tom Robertson's *Caste* in the 1860s, there is not one single play which would find its way today into the repertoire of a classical theatre; but many were the famous actors and actresses who either in their beginnings or in their maturity worked with the Macreadys at Bristol. The list includes Grimaldi, Foote, Fanny and Charles Kemble, Edmund and Charles Kean, Jenny Lind, the Bancrofts, Madge Kendal, Henry Irving and, above all, Ellen Terry, who joined Mr. Chute at the age of fourteen—when she had already been on the stage for five years! In 1867 James Henry Chute built the Princes Theatre (to be destroyed by bombs in 1940), but during his lifetime he clung to the management of both theatres. It was his son, James Macready Chute, who, succeeding his father, decided to devote himself solely to the new theatre, and he finally severed the family connection with the 'Old' Theatre in 1881. Incidentally, this James Macready Chute died in 1912, and was succeeded as Director of the Princes Theatre by his widow, who lived to become a grand old lady and a legendary figure among Bristol playgoers. Her death in 1931 marked the end of the hundred-and-thirteen-year connection between the Macready family and the Bristol theatres.

In the meantime, owing to the rise of the Princes Theatre, the Theatre Royal had lost its function. The whole system of stock companies began to die out all over the country, concurrently with the rise of cheap railway transport, and from the 1880s onwards, until it was killed by the rise of the cinema in the 1920s, the touring system from London flourished and prospered. As far as Bristol was concerned, the principal companies naturally went to the Princes Theatre, and the 'Old', as it was now universally called, passed into a state of decline. By now it stood in an area that was entirely dock and slum, and it was separated from the life of the new Bristol by an arm of the harbour.

In a map of 1910, the district of King Street and Queen's Square, once the hub of the city, appears as a small isolated peninsula of a vast, spreading town. Surrounded on three sides by the harbour, only a few narrow lanes lead to contact with the wider town at Baldwin Street. In the 1930s, the western leg of the harbour was filled in, and transformed into what is now the handsome Bristol Centre, and thus contact between the theatre and the citizens of Bristol was re-established. In the meantime the theatre, relying more and more on a dockside audience and on the sale of beer in its capacious bars, had degenerated into a home of third-rate variety and pantomime.

It passed through a succession of managements, and, in common with the rest of the theatrical world, it prospered a little during the 1914-18 war. In the postwar slump, Miss Muriel Pratt, who had been an Ibsen actress with J. T. Grein's Contemporary Theatre in London, tried to convert the 'Old' into a home for the new rising fashion of repertory, but with little success. Once more the theatre was on the market, and this time it was on the brink of being converted into a bacon factory. Vague rumours were afloat that the elders of the city would bestir themselves to preserve their treasure, but again it was left to private enterprise, and Douglas Millar took over in 1924 on behalf of the new owners Milton Bode and Robert Courtneidge. The theatre was by now almost derelict, its structure was deteriorating, and gallant though Mr. Millar's struggle was, little money could be set aside for internal improvement or decoration. In the next fifteen years it offered repertory, inferior touring companies, the cheapest kind of variety, but it was kept in existence by the reputation of its yearly pantomime, which ran for several months and, thanks to the new system of coach tours, attracted a wide, chiefly working-class audience from the whole of the West of England. The second war came and Fortescue's Repertory was in possession. The last play to be produced before the theatre was closed by the blitz was *Ignorance*, billed in thick type as 'For Adults Only'.

Miraculously it survived the blitz and stood out like an island in a sea of desolation. A few incendiary bombs fell on the roof and were put out by the fireman, who still works in the theatre as an attendant. The Princes had been wiped out, and although three other theatres in the town still functioned, the 'old' theatre stood forlorn and empty for eighteen months. The hungry eyes of merchants deprived of their own buildings fell upon it. In the decades before the war the dockside wholesale vegetable market had expanded around King Street and Charlotte Street; the fruiterers had already swallowed the handsome Coopers' Hall. It was natural that they should also covet the Theatre Royal.

History was repeating itself—first threatened with conversion into a boxing booth, then into a bacon factory, and now into a vegetable store.

History repeated itself on the converse side also. Once more kind friends came to the rescue. The theatre was put up for auction and was bought by an anonymous purchaser for £10,000, only twice the sum that it had cost to build one hundred and seventy-five years before. The purchaser remained anonymous for fourteen years; only on the occasion of the tenth anniversary of the Bristol Old Vic Company, in February 1956, was it revealed that his name was Mr. Clarence Davey, the managing director of a local metal firm. (He lives today in South Africa.) He offered to sell the building to any responsible body of citizens in the town for the same sum he had paid for it, on condition that the building was maintained as a theatre.

Herbert Farjeon, the dramatist, had written a letter to *The Times*, which had stirred the civic conscience. A small group of people began to busy themselves. Prominent among them were Wilfred Leighton, the Secretary of Bristol Municipal Charities, Robert Lyne, an alderman of the city, his wife, Veronica Lyne, and Cyril Wood, afterwards the regional director for C.E.M.A. and the Arts Council in the West of England. It is curious how tradition was maintained. The theatre had been built in 1766, against the opposition of the Puritans, largely through the determination of Alexander Organ, who subsequently became Mayor of the city. It was saved in 1942, despite the indifference of the multitude, largely through the determination of Robert Lyne, who subsequently became Lord Mayor of the city.

The Committee formed by Mr. Leighton found that it could expect little from the commercial theatre. The hard fact was that the building was not a commercial proposition. Had this not been the case—and this should be remembered in view of the minor controversies which have arisen during the past fourteen years—the business magnates of the theatre world would never have allowed it to pass into the hands of the Arts Council and the Old Vic. From their point of view the theatre stood in a slum, it would need an immense amount of money to put it right; and owing to the small seating capacity it would be almost impossible to regain the initial outlay. The seating capacity at that time was about one thousand. In order to comply with safety regulations,

17

it was reduced by C.E.M.A. to about seven hundred, and it is interesting to note that with one gallery less, in 1766, it had been claimed to hold accommodation for sixteen hundred people. When during the course of the alterations in 1943, this was pointed out to the Superintendent of Police, he could only throw up his hands with a shudder of horror.

The committee formed themselves into a body of trustees and set about trying to raise the money. An appeal was launched. Robert Donat was lured to Bristol and addressed a meeting in the Theatre Royal. The National Trust was persuaded to give a small donation. It was not an easy time, in the summer of 1942, to embark upon such a venture. The war was at its height. In the Western Desert, at Stalingrad, in the Battle of the Atlantic, the Allies were faring badly. Yet, perhaps, it is only in such moments that men turn their minds to the abnormal—and to the average British citizen the idea of a publicly endowed theatre was abnormal. One way and another, almost to the surprise of Mr. Leighton and his friends, £5,000 was collected. Another £5,000 was still needed.

It was Cyril Wood who broached the idea of appealing to the recently formed organisation, C.E.M.A. This body, whose full title was the Council for the Encouragement of Music and the Arts, was a wartime organisation, founded in the first place by the Pilgrim Trust, subsequently financed jointly with the Ministry of Education and afterwards taken over entirely by the Ministry. After the war this body was transposed into the present Arts Council of Great Britain, with its duty of developing the arts, but its immediate wartime task was to bring the joy of good entertainment to the civilian population suffering from the strain of conflict. Lord Keynes had been appointed chairman in the spring of 1942, and it was his vision and his influence which eventually ensured the postwar permanency of this wartime emergency instrument. From the first moment of his appointment, he worked with a view to attaining that permanency. His work as an expert on finance and economy was well known to the public; his deep interest in the arts and his love of the theatre were known only to a limited number.

It was Herbert Farjeon, then a member of the C.E.M.A. Drama Panel, who had first drawn the attention of Lord Keynes to the Bristol Theatre. Farjeon had stumbled by accident on the theatre in its worst 'slum' days in the 1930s. He had been very intrigued by it, had delved into its history, had broadcast and written about it, and had even tried, with the co-operation of Tyrone Guthrie, to arrange a special fortnight of classical plays within this historic setting. However, after a very amusing correspondence with the commercial owners, Bode and Courtneidge, he had given up that immediate idea, but readily flung himself into the breach as soon as the theatre came into the market.

Lord Keynes, therefore, had been well primed. He, himself, had made a great success of the Cambridge Arts Theatre, which he had founded and helped to endow just before the war, and the idea of being helpful in saving the oldest theatre in the country was one that inspired him. Basing his experience on Cambridge, he was confident that the theatrical magnates were wrong and that the theatre could be restored to its former dignity and, at the same time, be run on a satisfactory financial basis. Only one meeting with the Bristol delegates was needed for him to reach the decision that C.E.M.A. would undertake the responsibility. He offered there and then to take a twenty-one years' lease of the theatre. The bank, he was sure, would lend the newly appointed trustees the necessary £5,000 on the strength of the lease. C.E.M.A. would undertake to restore the building, take over the management and all expenses of the theatre, and provide a company of players worthy of the setting. The first £5,000 profits would be devoted to paying off the loan to the bank, so that the trustees might own the building free of encumbrance. He was not perturbed by the fact that the money provided for C.E.M.A. by the Ministry of Education was for the provision of plays and players, and not really for investment in bricks and mortar. Safe in his secluded office in the Treasury, to which he had been appointed as almost supreme financial adviser, he felt himself to be above any petty considerations. When his colleagues at the Treasury did find out some months later what had been happening and voiced some mild complaints, he laughed the matter off and, to put things right, wrote an article in *The Times*, which appeared on the day of the reopening of the theatre. In this article he admitted quite frankly that the whole proceeding might have been slightly irregular, but claimed that the opening of the first State-supported theatre in the country had come about in a 'typically haphazard English way'.

He was right about the bank. They did lend the money, though they were not pleased to find, at a slightly later date, that Lord Keynes had inserted an escape clause, by virtue of which C.E.M.A., at any time before the end of the war, could give six months' notice to terminate its contract. Not that Lord Keynes had any intention of using that clause. He would have been deeply pained if the necessity had arisen. One of his arguments, by which he urged the twenty-one years' lease on to his fellow councillors of C.E.M.A. was that it gave the organisation a continuity and would lend added weight to the postwar demands for putting C.E.M.A. on a permanent basis.

The trustees thus became, and still are, the actual owners of the building. They were for many years a loose body of individuals, but round about 1952 their position was legalised by a charter. The governing body now consists of the survivors of the original committee, amongst whom Mr. Leighton, the chairman, is still happily numbered. Added to them are delegates from the Bristol Corporation, the Arts Council, the National Trust, Bristol University, the Georgian Society and other kindred bodies. The lease held by C.E.M.A. was duly taken over by the Arts Council, and as long as this lease runs (it expires in 1963) the trustees have no financial responsibility.

I was at the time assistant drama director of C.E.M.A. and Lord Keynes appointed me to be general manager of the theatre. I was to be responsible for setting the theatre in order and running the companies. I took over my duties on November 1st, 1942, and the theatre reopened on May 11th, 1943.

The original repairs cost in the region of £8,000. Any doubts in the minds of those concerned as to whether the work would be permitted in wartime were quickly dispelled. Lord Keynes flashed the licences through the Ministry in the twinkling of an eye. No structural alterations were undertaken, for two reasons—the one because it was desired to economise in wartime, and the other because the trustees felt that it was their duty to preserve the original form of the building. Today, of course, the building having been scheduled as an 'ancient monument', no structural alteration may be put in hand without the permission of the Ministry of Works. The only real alteration undertaken in those initial operations was to the sunken Georgian pit, which, with its level floor and wooden benches, was converted into a sloping floor with tip-up fauteuil seats and renamed 'the stalls'. At the request of Mr. Carter, the Superintendent of Police, the seating in the gallery was reduced by about three hundred, and the management gladly acquiesced, because what the police call 'security' the theatre manager calls 'comfort for the patrons'. The wings of the gallery were railed off, and beyond the railing the original eighteenth-century seatings can still be seen, preserved as museum pieces. Despite all blandishments from Lord Keynes, the trustees refused to allow any alterations to the eighteenth-century structure behind-stage. Here, on the credit side, is the unique 'star trap' and elevator system, and the thunder roll in the roof. On the debit side are the shallow 'flies' and 'catwalks', which make it impossible to set up any scenery of a greater height than seventeen feet. This renders the theatre unsuitable for the sets of the average London touring company.

On the question of decoration, the last word in regard to the Theatre Royal will never be said. The theatre man who is concerned only with his own stagecraft knows that there can be copious but genuine disagreements between him and his fellow craftsmen; that modern thought may be divided into different schools, but nevertheless there is agreement on the basic principles. That same theatre man, if he has been connected with the Theatre Royal in Bristol, will have noted that no two experts on the subject have ever been able to agree on the correct interior decoration for the Theatre Royal. There have always been as many colour schemes as there have been experts. Maybe they are all right, for who can say what is the traditional décor of the theatre? Michael Edkins, in 1766, conceived it in green and gold. Palmer, we know, made copious alterations about 1800, so did Macready in 1820, and his son-in-law, James Henry Chute, thirty years later, 're-decorated, papered, painted, ornamented and re-gilded'. When C.E.M.A. took over in 1942, the panels surrounding the pit (stalls) were painted in hideous pink and cream, the work of Douglas Millar in 1924. The panels themselves, with their embossed decorations, were mid-Victorian, created by the order of Chute, yet underneath each panel there lie two other layers. One of these is an early Victorian canvas, with crude allegorical paintings, and below that lies the plain woodwork of Michael Edkins, on which traces of the original green and gold can still be seen—on those specimens that have been uncovered at times.

Two of the canvas panels from the middle layer are now on exhibition in the upper circle foyer.

Wilfred Leighton, the chairman of the trustees, who, since he has made a close study of the subject, is perhaps the most reliable expert, rebuts the idea that there is any traditional décor for the theatre to which it is imperative to revert. The theatre, he declares, is a palimpsest, and it is the primary duty of the trustees to preserve that palimpsest; and as long as Mr. Leighton is chairman of the trustees he is likely to have the last word.

In 1942 the architect was Ralph Edwards, well known in the West Country, who held the position until 1950, and he decided on a colour scheme mainly based on the original green and gold. And certainly, on the opening night in May 1943, the theatre, with its star-spangled ceiling, its Doric, fluted pillars, its unique horse-shoe shape, was a thing of beauty. Nor does any other colour scheme detract from the effect. Today Eustace Button, equally well known in Bristol, is the architect. The seats in the stalls and dress circle are now maroon. The eighteenth-century woodwork at the back of the dress circle matches them in colour. The gold has been enhanced, the green made secondary. The ceiling still sparkles, and the total effect is again one of rare beauty.

Once the building was ready for use, the future policy of the theatre had to be determined. It had at first been thought that the Old Vic, which had recently taken over the Liverpool Playhouse, might extend its activities to Bristol. They were running a classical repertory in the long-established theatre in Liverpool, which had been vacated in wartime by its directors, and the suggestion was raised that they might run the Theatre Royal, in conjunction with C.E.M.A., for a similar purpose. However, the administrators, Tyrone Guthrie and Bronson Albery, decided that their commitments at the time would not allow them to embark upon any new venture. Lord Keynes was not in the least dismayed by this turn of events. From the first, and to the last, he felt that the policy of the theatre should be the presentation of superb companies from the Metropolis, and that the function of C.E.M.A. should be to subsidise these companies against the inevitable loss that would result. He would even have liked to include opera; and his drama panel, the chief members of which were Herbert Farjeon, Ashley Dukes and J. B. Priestley, had some difficulty in dissuading him from the idea that the opening night should be a gala performance of Sadler's Wells Opera in an elaborate production of *Figaro*. This production was to be financed by the Cambridge Arts Theatre Trust, of which Lord Keynes was the chairman.

Eventually, after much discussion, it was decided that for the first six weeks the Old Vic were to present plays on the usual commercial sharing terms with C.E.M.A. After that it would be the duty of the general manager to select existing companies of the highest possible standard, giving preference to those in association with C.E.M.A. The Old Vic also undertook to return for short periods at stated intervals.

Mr. T. C. P. Hickson (popularly known as 'Tom') had been appointed as resident manager. He had been for twenty years (up to the day of its destruction) the manager of the Princes Theatre, and his appointment to the Theatre Royal has proved a blessing for the last fourteen years. A man of infinite resource and worldly wisdom, Tom knows everybody in the town, and everybody knows him, and his personality in the front of the house has helped to cement a faithful audience.

The opening play chosen by the Old Vic was one in keeping with the history of the theatre—*She Stoops to Conquer*. This play had been written nine years after the theatre had been built, and within months of its first production at Covent Garden it had been produced by Powel's company at the Theatre Royal in Bristol. C.E.M.A. had been touring a production of the play, under the management of Stanford Holme, to the hostels in the dispersed wartime factories, and this production, by Dorothy Green, was taken over by the Old Vic, refurbished, and given a new décor. Sybil Thorndike (playing Mrs. Hardcastle) was added to the cast, which already included Thea Holme, O. B. Clarence and Stanford Holme.

The opening night was one of the most festive in the history of the wartime British theatre. All the critics of the London Press came down to Bristol, and were accompanied by several well-known theatre people such as Sir Barry Jackson, Herbert Farjeon and Bronson Albery. Lord and Lady Keynes were of course resplendent in the Royal Box, which bears the coat of arms of George the Third. The Mayor, the Sheriffs, the *élite* of Clifton and Bristol (what Macready would surely have described as 'the gentry of the town') were present in bulk. The B.B.C. had made a great occasion of the evening, and devoted a full half-hour to the

23

opening ceremony—a rare concession in wartime. First came Laurence Housman, on behalf of the West of England, welcoming the new venture; then came some eighteenth-century music played by the Jacques Orchestra in the theatre pit, and this was followed by Sybil Thorndike, who, in front of the curtain, delivered a gracefully written and witty prologue, prepared by Herbert Farjeon (see Appendix). The first two or three minutes of the play concluded the broadcast.

The evening was exciting. The production was good, though not outstanding. It played for a fortnight to absolute capacity, and was followed by a production of a new play, *Queen Bee* by Judith Guthrie, produced by Hugh Miller. This was not so successful, but interest was reawakened by Bridie's *Susannah and the Elders*, which was brought down from Liverpool. Nova Pilbeam played Susannah and the producer was John Moody, who thus made his first contact with the Theatre Royal.

This concluded the first six weeks of the Old Vic, and by this time it was evident that the theatre was going to be a success. The vast publicity, both national and local, given to the venture had brought a public to the theatre and attracted the very necessary support of the middle classes. Thousands of Bristolians who had lived all their lives in the city were visiting the theatre for the first time, or, in the case of middle-aged, respectable citizens, were revisiting it for the first time since in their student days they had taken part in some Saturday-night rag in the sunken Georgian pit. That was the sort of local reputation that the theatre had enjoyed for the previous decades.

The Old Vic Company was followed by the Ballet Jooss, by six weeks of Norman Marshall's Company, by the Ballet Rambert, by Robert Atkins's Shakespearian Company from Regent's Park, and a season of Shaw. By this time the supply of goodish companies was thinning out, and the specially assembled C.E.M.A. companies which were touring the war workers' hostels had to be brought into the Theatre Royal. Towards the end of the year 1943 the theatre again reached the news with a first production of a new Priestley play *Desert Highway*. This was presented by A.B.C.A., the Army Play Unit, which was composed of professional actors then in the Services. Sir Philip Morris, subsequently the Vice-Chancellor of Bristol University, and chairman of the Bristol Old Vic Management Committee, was a director of A.B.C.A. (the Army Bureau of Current Affairs), and Michael MacOwan was the producer of the play. This was the first introduction to the Theatre Royal of two men who were to play an important part in its future.

Desert Highway, which attracted to its first night not only the national Press but also an imposing array of Red Tabs from the War Office, was subsequently presented at the Playhouse in London, where it had quite a long run. J. B. Priestley had been present at the final rehearsals and at the first night. As a result, a year or so later he wrote a very gripping play about an old historic theatre whose Green Room was haunted by the ghost of a young actress. This play was *Jenny Villiers*, which was given its first production by the Bristol Old Vic Company in 1946.

For the Christmas season of 1943 to the early spring of 1944 the theatre was given over to the Travelling Repertory Theatre Company. This was a wartime creation of which Basil Langton, a product of the Michel St. Denis Studio in Islington in the nineteen-thirties, was the founder and director.

Langton was an attractive and serious young actor, and he gathered around him several young and promising artists—among them Paul Scofield, Renée Asherson and Ann Casson. In his first season at Bristol he put on a special production of *Romeo and Juliet*, with himself as Romeo, Jeannette Tregarthen as Juliet and Paul Scofield as Mercutio. In the following year he presented a spectacular production of *St. Joan*, in which Anne Casson played Joan. This production, after leaving Bristol, was taken for a prolonged tour of Great Britain and then to Germany, being one of the first companies to play in that country after VE day.

The first twelve months of C.E.M.A.'s management of the theatre ended with another visit of an Old Vic company—this time the production was *Guilty*, an adaptation of Zola's play, in which Flora Robson played Thérèse Raquin. On the financial side, the year had been an eminently successful one, as over £7,000 profit had been made, and almost the whole of the initial costs of renovation had been paid off. But, although the profits did not dwindle, from that time forward the standards began to deteriorate.

The Old Vic sent no further companies. Walter Hudd, who, for the sake of his social conscience, had ignored the rewarding

25

financial career that would have been open to him in a West End war-starved of actors, and had served C.E.M.A. in the hostels for years, brought his company to Bristol for several weeks in the summer of 1944. The drooping standard was raised again, but the supply could not spread over fifty-two weeks. Various repertory companies from all over the country were invited to play for a week or two in the theatre. They were successful in attracting an audience, but their standard was no better than that of the gallant Little Theatre at the Colston Hall, and there was obviously no justification for creating such a competition. In spite of all this, the second financial year showed a profit of nearly £6,000.

In the summer of 1945, after VE day, came the first slump. Alec Clunes, then at the height of his success at the Arts Theatre in London, took a company to Bristol for six weeks. The plays included a new production of *Hamlet*, which was afterwards to be greatly applauded in London. Business was deplorable. It was true that, at the time, the theatre was suffering all over the country, except in the Metropolis, which was still crowded with troops and missions from every part of the world; but all the usual box-office excuses could not account for the failure of a season which, twelve months before, would have crowded the theatre.

The truth had to be faced. The theatre had been renovated and made to look beautiful. It was no longer a building in which the citizen of Bristol was ashamed to be seen—but it had no policy, and without a policy it could not retain a faithful public. The problem, in spite of the difference in material surroundings, was the same as that which had confronted Douglas Millar and his colleagues in the fifteen years preceding the war. The theatre was too small, both in its stage facilities and in the seating capacities, to attract touring companies of first-class standard. Also there had been a special wartime audience, with a large sprinkling of American soldiers. Those conditions no longer prevailed, the public no longer felt excited at the prospect of visiting the Theatre Royal, and when a first-class company like that of Alec Clunes did appear it took two or three weeks of word of mouth before the unbelievers could be persuaded that it was worth their while to take up the theatregoing habit again.

No one had been more conscious of this than I, the general manager. I had warned the drama panel in the spring of 1945 that, although profits were still good, the lack of policy would at the end be fatal. But Lord Keynes made it clear that he thought it would be better to sacrifice some of the profits and engage more expensive companies. He would not believe that it could not be possible to induce leading and star actors to come to the theatre if they were given sufficient financial inducement. His aim was that one should be able to see continually, at the Theatre Royal in Bristol, companies as good as would be seen in a long run at the Haymarket Theatre in London. He did not believe that such a result could be obtained from a resident company in Bristol.

In the summer of 1945, after the failure of Clunes's company, it was evident that matters could not be allowed to continue as they were. I approached Guthrie, then still the administrator. It had been a bitter disappointment when, before the reopening of the theatre, Guthrie had withdrawn from the original plan of establishing an Old Vic Company at Bristol. It was gratifying to learn that his views had now changed, and he was prepared to consider a scheme. He himself was about to leave the Old Vic, but he handed the discussion over to his successor, John Burrell, who was whole-heartedly in favour of the idea.

Michael MacOwan had, in the meantime, become Drama Director of C.E.M.A. (by then the Arts Council). Macowan was at once convinced that the Arts Council would no longer be justified in holding any responsibility at the Theatre Royal unless this or some similar scheme were put into action. Discussions were held with John Burrell and with George Chamberlain, the general manager of the Old Vic. A draft agreement was arranged with Chamberlain. Under this agreement, the Old Vic was to be responsible for the company, the Arts Council for the theatre, and the Old Vic was, in addition, to receive a guarantee of its expenses from the Arts Council.

It was now time to acquaint Lord Keynes with the plans that were on foot. I wrote him a nine-page letter. In this I clearly set out all that had been accomplished; I spoke of the gradual deterioration of the companies available and of the dwindling support. I told the noble lord about the grumblings and mumblings that were beginning to be heard among the people who mattered in the town. C.E.M.A. had accomplished a fine job in Bristol; the Arts Council could only consolidate that work by establishing a permanent company of the highest standard. I was convinced that it was the function of the Theatre Royal to return to its great days, when it had housed the stock companies and given early training and experience to young actresses such as Sarah Siddons and Ellen Terry. I concluded by giving Lord Keynes an outline of the discussions that had so far taken place with the Old Vic, and submitted the draft contract.

Lord Keynes's reply was frigid in the extreme. He still did not believe in the policy of a resident company. Motivated, no doubt, by justifiable pride in the new-born Arts Council, which owed its very existence to his insight and imagination, he thought it was defeatist to assume, at so early a stage in the history of the Council, that it was not in the position to develop its own policies and its own companies. However, if this was the considered advice of his two drama directors, he was open to conviction that it might be wiser, as a *temporary* measure, to depute the responsibilities to another body. The draft contract met with his complete disapproval. Other financial methods would have to be found.

Shortly afterwards Lord Keynes departed to America for the last of his Lease-Lend talks. The negotiations continued in his absence. He was kept informed about their progress, but although, in his replies to the secretary-general of the Arts Council, he acknowledged the information, his attitude did not change. It is possible that, had he been in England in the autumn of 1945 and able to devote his attention to the matter, the Bristol Old Vic Company might never have come into existence.

Agreement was reached whilst he was still in America. The financial policy was eventually solved by an arrangement that the Arts Council would be entirely responsible for all expenses—whilst losses over a certain amount were to be met by the Old Vic. The new company—to be called the Bristol Old Vic Company—was to be directed by the Old Vic, but jointly managed, as far as finance was concerned, by the two parent bodies. The theatre building was to be managed solely by the Council. Lord Keynes returned to England a few days before the opening of the Company, and he died two months later. He had only once visited the theatre —on the occasion of its reopening by C.E.M.A. in 1943—but he always took an intense personal interest in its progress. A weekly report was sent to him, and often he would return it with copious notes. He was indeed proud of its financial success and the national publicity which it attracted, and he was extremely grateful, and very kind, to all those whom he considered to have been in any way responsible for that success. As he had no personal contact with the theatre and the city, he could not reconcile the management's gloomy forebodings of the future with the rosy picture presented by the balance-sheet. Let no one, however, underestimate the part played both by Lord Keynes and by C.E.M.A. in the history of the Theatre Royal, Bristol. It was his vision that caused C.E.M.A. to step in at the crucial moment and give the financial assistance that enabled the trustees to save the theatre. It was C.E.M.A., under the guidance of Lord Keynes, which carried out a wartime policy that brought distinction to the Theatre Royal, enjoyment to the citizens of a war-stricken city, and, at the same time, laid a solid foundation, on which the Bristol Old Vic was eventually to be built. [C.L.]

CHAPTER TWO

The First Season
1946

THE OLD VIC, under their agreement with the Arts Council had the responsibility of appointing a director for the new company, and John Burrell, as the administrator of the Old Vic, finally decided upon Hugh Hunt.

Hunt, at that time, was thirty-five years old. He had been during the five war years in Intelligence, where he had much to do with the training and dispatch of British agents to occupied France —a fluent and almost native command of French is one of his non-theatrical assets. President of O.U.D.S. in the early nineteen-thirties, his prewar theatrical career had been a remarkable one for so young a man. After a short period at Croydon Repertory Theatre he became director at the Westminster, where his most notable production, and one that is still remembered in theatrical annals, was *King Lear*, with William Devlin in the title role. Both actor and producer were only twenty-four years old, and although Devlin was to repeat his performance under other direction at the Old Vic in the following year, during the whole of the nineteen-thirties there was only one other performance of *Lear* in London— that of John Gielgud, also at the Old Vic, in 1931. His reputation established, Hunt moved to Dublin, where for three years, from 1935 to 1938, he was director at the Abbey Theatre. Here he soon made his own definite impression, producing, during his period of office, over thirty original Irish plays, the most noted of which were Paul Vincent Carroll's *Shadow and Substance* and Denis Johnston's *Blind Man's Buff*. The beginning of the war found him free-lancing in London and preparing a production of *Shadow and Substance* for the West End, but this had to be abandoned.

In many ways, therefore, the appointment of this young man to lead this new young company was an ideal one. Shy and retiring at first acquaintance, Hugh Hunt nevertheless possesses a tenacity of purpose which has served him well in the vicissitudes that have beset his career during the eleven years that have elapsed since his nomination as the director of the Bristol Old Vic in the autumn of 1945. From the outset he knew that the position would not be an easy one and that he would have to thread his way carefully between the sometimes conflicting views of his two masters—the Old Vic and the Arts Council. There were strong personalities concerned in both organisations, and it says much for Hugh Hunt that, though he himself was at times involved in the differences of opinion, he was always faithful to his artistic integrity and he never wavered from the furtherance of the ambition which he had announced at the first public meeting at Bristol—the determination to make the new company not a junior partner, but the equal of the Old Vic in the Waterloo Road.

This first meeting took place in the office of the Theatre Royal in December 1945. As already stated, there had been a rising discontent amongst the Press and the citizens of Bristol at the low standard of fare offered at the theatre. Foremost and most formidable amongst the 'discontents' had been Mr. John Garrett, the headmaster of Bristol Grammar School, himself a noted Shakespearian authority, a lecturer and broadcaster, and a contributor of articles on the theatre to such papers as *The Spectator*.

Michael MacOwan, as drama director of the Arts Council, in a few well-chosen words, spoke of his awareness of the feeling in the town, although he was careful to add 'we don't stand here in sackcloth and ashes'. He then outlined the new plans which had been arrived at between the Arts Council and the Old Vic, and introduced the new director.

Hugh Hunt straight away made an indelible impression on the assembled gathering, and the Bristol Press took him to their hearts. From the outset the support of the Bristol newspapers, the *Western Daily Press*, the *Bristol Evening Post*, the *Bristol Evening World*, has been one of the greatest assets that the Bristol Old Vic Company has possessed. They have been keen in their interest and candid in their comments. They have given great praise when they thought it deserved, and not hesitated to be scathing when they thought such criticism to be called for. It is no exaggeration to say there is no other provincial city in Great Britain where so much space is devoted by the local Press to its repertory theatre. Hunt detailed his ambitions, his programme of plays and his leading artists, who were to include William Devlin and Pamela Brown. He spoke hesitatingly and with not very great enthusiasm about the length of the run of each play. The considered opinion of the administration at that time was that there would not be a public in Bristol for more than two weeks for each play. It had therefore been decided that, whilst it was necessary for the purpose of maintaining a standard to allow three weeks' rehearsal for each production, the third week would be played at the neighbouring towns of Bath and Weston-super-Mare. A series of dates had been booked for the spring at the theatres in these two towns, and it had been arranged that the company should rehearse in Bristol during the day-time and be taken to and from the 'touring date' by coach in the evening. During the week that the company were in Bath or Weston the theatre would be filled by a ballet company or by a visit from the Company of Four from the Lyric Theatre, Hammersmith. Hunt said quite frankly that he did not think that this was an ideal arrangement, and he stated firmly that his first aim as director would be to try to create a public which would enable each play to run in the theatre for the necessary three weeks. He pledged himself to his audience to work towards that ideal, and Mr. Garrett, as spokesman, pledged the support of the theatregoers of Bristol. He welcomed Hugh Hunt, recalled with pleasure the production of *King Lear* with Devlin in 1934, and hoped that Bristol might see that production again. On that happy note the meeting ended.

On February 19th, 1946, the Bristol Old Vic Company was inaugurated with Hugh Hunt's production of Farquhar's *The Beaux' Stratagem*. Christopher Hassall had written a special prologue.[1]   [C.L.]

Obviously it was important that the opening production should attract attention and set a promising standard for the future, and the London press, as on many occasions in later years, was invited to see the work of the Bristol Old Vic. The company certainly aimed high; and apart from Pamela Brown and William Devlin, the Mrs. Sullen and Archer, included Faith Brook, Yvonne Mitchell, Nora Nicholson, Noel Willman, Robert Sansom and Kenneth Connor—names either already known to London critics and playgoers or to be known by them widely in the future.

On the whole, critical response was more than encouraging.

[1] Christopher Hassall's Prologue. See Appendix B.

'They come fairly triumphantly out of this test', wrote Lionel Hale. 'That is not to say that this is the perfect performance of *The Beaux' Stratagem*, but it is a performance that shows all the right motives and very many of the right achievements.' 'The light and lovely touch' of Hugh Hunt's production was praised, with its 'tinklings of Scarlatti' (the music, by Karl Haas, was played by the London Baroque Quintet) and Tanya Moiseiwitsch's décor with its richly beautiful draped curtain in the bedroom scene. And the company itself won honours, although opinion was divided about Pamela Brown's Mrs. Sullen. 'This is potentially our best young actress', wrote Hale. 'She is here bitty and piecey, with increasing mannerisms and affectations such as a rippling laugh growing on her.' Ivor Brown, on the other hand, welcomed her fresh touch in Restoration comedy. 'Miss Pamela Brown plays Lady Sullen with every weapon that stars in costume plays do not use, quietude, sincerity, and the charm of a red squirrel. She employs none of those they do use. Not for her the over-stressing, the rolling eye, the laboured mischief in pointing a risky line. She is right to go her own way and not to set up in the traditional line of business. Farquhar might have thought her a trifle tame; but I find this sort of acting memorable where flashier things fade.'

William Devlin, a natural tragedian, was generally considered to have assumed the alien personality of Archer with skill, and everywhere Kenneth Connor attracted attention: 'a new and admirable clown'; 'a low comedian of rare qualities'. Robert Sansom's 'delicately pointed speaking of the prologue' was also admired; an interesting transformation for those who remembered his admirable direct and staunch airman Streeter in *Thunder Rock* with Michael Redgrave early in the war.

On March 13th, 1946, the company presented its first new play: J. B. Priestley's *Jenny Villiers*, the appropriate 'story of a theatre; an old theatre full of traditions, in which the great actors and actresses of the past played—a Theatre Royal. A modern repertory company have come to this theatre to play a new play. The author, left alone in the Green Room, sees the ghosts of a company who played there in 1840 and learns from the young leading actress the lesson that the theatre never dies, but has in it the seeds of its own regeneration'.

'Bristol is the most favoured city in the country so far as the

33

theatre is concerned', Priestley had declared. 'I want people here to realise what a magnificent thing this Old Vic venture is.' His play, nevertheless, had not been specially written for the Bristol Theatre Royal, and it was in part a new variation on the time theory. The cynical and bitter author (Devlin) who contacts an actress of one hundred years before in the theatre Green Room carries echoes, moreover, of the heroes of *Thunder Rock* and *Berkeley Square*, and like them he moves in the clothes of today among the people of a past century. The *Western Daily Press* considered it 'a superb and daring play', but although *The Times* thought the story 'an enthralling one' it qualified with the remark that 'From end to end of the play there is not a single phrase or turn of thought capable of working magic'. 'Nor', it added, 'is there a single phrase which is not good theatre.' 'His words and the quality of his thought remain doggedly spry and prosaic', echoed Philip Hope-Wallace.

Yet the play theatrically held the stage, and Hugh Hunt's production, with its use of a wandering spotlight, did much to suggest the enchanted movement outside time. 'William Devlin plays the sick dramatist sardonically and well', wrote *The Observer*, 'and Pamela Brown, faced with the appalling task of combining Rose Trelawny, Mary Rose, and the younger Miss Pettigrew in *Berkeley Square*, quietly and breathtakingly combines them.' For Hope-Wallace, too, the actress had 'an exquisite, unworldly radiance'. Faith Brook's outstanding performance as a modern girl, Pauline Fraser, was notably praised, and Hugh Hunt took his place as actor in the company with unintentional celerity—deputising for Robert Sansom at short notice owing to Sansom's illness.

Macbeth, the Bristol Old Vic's first Shakespearian production, had been an ambition of Hugh Hunt and William Devlin from the start of the venture. The cast today reads most interestingly: Devlin as Macbeth, Pamela Brown as Lady Macbeth, Noel Willman as Banquo, Robert Sansom as Macduff, Kenneth Connor as the Porter, Faith Brook as Lady Macduff and Nora Nicholson and Yvonne Mitchell as first and second witches.

Hunt's production was 'three-dimensional', filling not only the length and breadth but also the height of the stage, a construction which added a fierce excitement to the final fight of Macbeth and Macduff, when Devlin leapt from the top to the middle rostrum only to be pierced by his enemy's sword and fall to his death on the stage beneath. The settings were by Guy Sheppard—'miraculously atmospheric and lovely' wrote John Bennett of the *Bristol Evening World*—and both the music and production were praised for 'wildness and passion'.

Pamela Brown's Lady Macbeth has still, ten years later, to be seen in London, but at Bristol it set its mark on theatre history: 'a very cobra of a woman with an insinuating poison, and passion with a very capital "P" ', wrote the *Western Daily Press*. In the murder scene there was, according to Bennett, 'full horror of the deed', ranging from 'almost whispered terror to Macbeth's hysterical outburst stilled by a totally unexpected but highly dramatic face-slap from Lady Macbeth'. John Garrett, too, was impressed by the development of the relationship between the two.

> The evil to which this tremendous pair have set their hands corrodes even their own love, and this production emphasises this in two memorable pictures. Macbeth and his 'dearest love' together in perfection of physical harmony; and only a few scenes later, after she has had to summon him to her, they stood not together but back to back, as he says over his shoulder: 'Thou know'st that Banquo and his Fleance live.'

> Mr. Hunt's production was full of such imaginative subtleties. Macbeth's shutting of the castle gates, excluding the forces which would have saved Duncan; Lady Macbeth's gesture of rolling up her sleeves as she was about to enter the room of death; the smashing of the window as the castle's citadel fell, were others. . . .

> Other excellences were the music, the really terrifying witches, the well-timed noises of bustle and shouting off-stage, a first-class Banquo and, of course, the richly satisfying performances of Pamela Brown and William Devlin.

Devlin's Macbeth, 'more kingly than the kings', reminded one critic of Hazlitt's description of the character: 'absent and per-plexed, sudden and desperate in act, from a distrust of his own resolution'. This noble-voiced and virile actor has achieved granite with the years, and a maturity which has to some degree replaced the feverish fire of impatience that consumed the stage of the Old Vic, ten years before, when—an actor never seemingly young—he came to early grips with Peer Gynt and Cassius, Leontes and Richard III. His Macbeth, after long wartime service, reopened a new range of Shakespearian portraits.

Some felt Kenneth Connor's Porter too Grock-like, but as a whole the cast caught the impact of the tragedy and production. It was Pamela Brown's last play for the company and her leaving was obviously a loss. Yvonne Mitchell, who succeeded her as a leading player, was too young and inexperienced to replace her, although she brought ripening talents and qualities of her own to the established team.

Macbeth, produced on April 10th, 1946, was followed on the 30th by Tchehov's *The Seagull*, which played to a loss. 'Getting guest artists to play occasionally will bring freshness to the company', Hugh Hunt had stated, and Lydia Sherwood and Jane Henderson therefore joined the company for this play as Madame Arkadina and Masha. Jane Henderson, five years before, had been an outstanding Yelena in *Uncle Vanya* at the Oxford Repertory, where she had distinguished herself as a character actress of considerable emotional depth. But it is possible that Lydia Sherwood, an actress with a strong right-hand punch, was not so happily cast in Tchehov and one critic saw in her performance 'more of Judith Bliss than Irina'. Garrett, on the other hand, welcomed the 'edge':

> Miss Sherwood's performance was as glitteringly perfect and complete as a diamond faultlessly cut. Her scene with her son Konstantin was perfectly played, and suggested Hamlet and Gertrude all over again. . . .
>
> Mr. Willman (Trigorin) was no match for Miss Sherwood. There was no force of compulsion in his conversational 'Oh, let me be free'; he never convinced us that he was caught irretrievably by Nina's young and innocent beauty. . . .

Where another critic, too, had felt the stylised setting distracting ('It must remain a mystery, unless the symbolism is beyond us, why the drawing-room ceiling was removed to show about four or five square yards of blue sky and tree tops'), Garrett was moved by 'the beauty of the groupings, Mr. Devlin's correctly endearing Sorin, the subtlety of Konstantin's touch at his previous scar as he goes out to kill himself'. The Konstantin was Patrick Troughton, and the dark-eyed, gazelle-nerved Yvonne

Mitchell had her first outstanding part as Nina. She 'fulfilled expectations and always seemed to have plenty of power in reserve', wrote Garrett.

Tchehov's play, a comedy with spring leaves swept by the blasts of winter, has wood-notes of tragedy. Bristol's next production, a world première, was described in a headline as 'almost farce'. The author of *Keep in a Cool Place*, W. P. Templeton, had been one of the team of writers responsible for *Exercise Bowler*, a wartime effort at the Arts Theatre which had attracted attention for originality. The new play was concerned with the difficulties of acclimatisation experienced by wartime brides at the Glenlannoch home of the McLeods, and gave Robert Sansom his longest part and greatest success of the season as Marcus, the father of the McLeods. It had, wrote John Bennett, 'some gloriously amusing lines and situations. Yet, despite a lovely character study by William Devlin, and despite the twinkle and the roguishness of Faith Brook, and despite the brave attempt of Robert Sansom to cope with the situations, *Keep in a Cool Place* won't, I fear, keep'. He added that it sagged badly after the second act and ventured the opinion that the author wrote the third swiftly—'probably with his eyes shut'.

It was a general verdict, although Garrett at least thought it a minor piece of a potential master, and elsewhere Templeton was coupled with Ustinov as one of our two most notable young dramatists.

The comedy was produced by William Devlin, while engaged in comparatively easy rehearsal for Orsino in Hunt's production of *Twelfth Night*. With settings and costumes by Tanya Moiseiwitsch, this opened on June 5th.

Four years later, in November 1950, Hunt was to produce the play as the opening production at the rehabilitated Old Vic Theatre in the Waterloo Road in London, and the same general criticism—his overstressing of the comedy—was to be made. 'In *Twelfth Night*', wrote John Garrett, 'Mr. Hugh Hunt seemed to have asked himself the question: "Now by what new twist can I jazz up this old play?" and to have answered it with disastrous results to Shakespeare.' He was handicapped, the writer added, 'by a set the complications of which had to be seen to be believed. Arches, steps, balconies, terraces, doorways. . . .' Others noted the limitations of movement, and the costumes though rich were also bulky and restrictive (Devlin later shed his Rembrandt 'tammy', but Viola in Jacobean breeches, with a plumed hat, cannot suggest the lithe boyishness and stripling grace of Cesario).

Hunt seems always to have been stirred by the comedy more than the poetry of this play, and the see-saw business—inventive and funny enough—of the 'drunken scene' of Aguecheek, Feste and Sir Toby was carried over from King Street to the Waterloo Road. In this sense his cast served him well: 'Robert Sansom's robustious Sir Toby bubbles with merriment', wrote Dennis Bushell of the *Bristol Evening World*, 'and Brian Haines's grinning, spindle-shanked Sir Andrew stands out as one of the most perfect memories of the evening.' Noel Willman's Malvolio was also popular with the audience, though Bushell felt he should have less bounce and more grave dignity, and also strictured Yvonne Mitchell for a 'tendency to recite rather than portray inner feeling and depth'. Kenneth Connor was the Feste, Faith Brook (as later with the Old Vic at the New Theatre) the Olivia, and Helen Burns, a clever little actress who had once played a first-class Nora in *A Doll's House*, the Maria.

Denis Johnston's new play about Swift, *Weep for the Cyclops*, was a matter of greater distinction. Produced on June 26th, 1946, it was the last play of the Bristol Old Vic season, and the interest it aroused was wide. Yet once again complete success evaded the modern author. ' "Something original, something alive, something adventurous" is printed on the programme as the aim of the Old Vic. This play is fully in accord with all three points. It is original, alive and adventurous. It is more. It is both stimulating and profoundly irritating', wrote the *Western Daily Press*.

The technique employed was unusual: the dramatist breaking the illusion from time to time by making his characters step out of the stage picture and become people acting in a play. Thornton Wilder and Jean Anouilh (in *The Lark*) have used similar methods with skill, and for some Johnston's daring device did not decrease the play's power. In one scene in which Swift broke off a discussion with Stella in order deliberately to exclude the vital secret of his private life which prevented his marrying her—these two missing pages of the script being inserted later into the last act— was, however, an invention of equivocal dramatic effect: intended to promote mystery or tension, it provoked from one critic the criticism of bad craftsmanship. Nevertheless, it was a play that was both provocative and alive: 'a brilliant play', wrote Dennis Bushell, 'vividly portraying the undying love of two women for a man who could scarcely be called normal . . . *Weep for the Cyclops* is a profound emotional experience'.

Its major triumph was Devlin's Swift, described by Bushell as 'eclipsing in sheer brilliance and depth any other performance he has given in Bristol'. 'The most brilliant character study which Bristol has seen for months—perhaps years', echoed the *Western Daily Press*. 'All else must give way to Mr. Devlin's majestic portrait.' There was reference, too, to the 'tender, moving Stella of Meriel Moore' (an actress from the Gate Theatre, Dublin, and later Devlin's wife) and Yvonne Mitchell's 'fine study of hysteria and desperation' as Vanessa. Hunt produced, with settings and costumes by Tanya Moiseiwitsch and Guy Sheppard.

The first Old Vic season ended on July 6th, although the company played a further two weeks at the Arts Theatre, Cambridge.

'This experiment is really of nation-wide importance', Devlin had said at a meeting of the Bristol Rotary Club in May, 'and is the test whether communities like Bristol are prepared to judge, criticise and support, by their own standard, and not on second-hand London standards.' And Hunt in two articles in the *Bristol Evening Post* in July and August had succinctly stated the policy: 'It is simply this—to present the great masterpieces of drama, as well as new plays of merit, in a style worthy of the great traditions of the British stage; and in such a fashion to ensure that the public can see a continuous flow of such plays, in contradistinction to the limited offerings presented by the long-run commercial theatre, whose main purpose is to make profits.'

In this first short season both ideals were aimed at and to a large degree attained; they set the note for the future, and the experiment of 'nation-wide importance' was born.   [A.W.]

CHAPTER THREE

The Second Season
1946 *to* 1947

IT WAS TOUCH AND GO whether the Bristol Old Vic Company would continue to exist after its first short season. Under the peculiar arrangement which had been set up between the two parent bodies, the Old Vic was responsible for the direction of the company, but they were jointly responsible with the Arts Council for the management, whilst the latter body were solely responsible for the finances. The loss on the period from February to July 1946 had been over £3,000. Lord Keynes had died in April, but his influence persisted, and it was remembered that he had been lukewarm and apprehensive about the formation of the company. Moreover, the Arts Council were still smarting over the failure of the West Riding Theatre venture, which had cost them £26,000 and brought very little in the way of prestige. Nor could they overlook the fact that it was the same two drama directors, MacOwan and Landstone, who had urged them to undertake both ventures. A joint meeting was held to consider the future at Bristol. In the chair was Sir Ernest Pooley, who had recently ceased to be a Governor of the Old Vic in order to succeed Lord Keynes as the Chairman of the Arts Council. In his somewhat ambiguous position he was falling over himself sideways in order to preserve an attitude of fairness and freedom from bias; but he was (and is) a shrewd old man, and he had the vision to see the possibilities of the company, although financially it had made so inauspicious a start. Almost imperceptibly, he guided the meeting to a favourable decision, tamed down his two fiery drama directors, and secured a reprieve for the company. The Arts Council was to continue to take the financial risk of the company up till the summer of 1947. Before that date was reached the tide had turned.

One important and far-reaching administrative decision was, however, reached at that meeting. It was decided to set up a management committee at Bristol, to be responsible to both parent

Photo by John Vickers

Photo by Derrick O. Michelson   *Photo by Angus McBean*

THE DIRECTORS
TOP: (left) Hugh Hunt (1946-9); (right) Allan Davis (1950).
BOTTOM: (left) Denis Carey (1950-4); (right) John Moody (1954-7).

The Beaux' Stratagem (Farquhar), 1946. L. *to* R. Pamela Brown, Faith Brook, Noël Willman (seated), William Devlin, Kenneth Connor, Nora Nicholson (seated). Setting and costumes by Tanya Moiseiwitsch.

Macbeth, 1946. Pamela Brown as Lady Macbeth.

An Inspector Calls (J. B. Priestley), 1946. Rosalie Crutchley as Sheila
Birling and William Devlin as Inspector Goole.

bodies for the running of the company. Both the Arts Council and the Old Vic were to be represented on this committee, and it was decided to ask Sir Philip Morris, the Vice-Chancellor of Bristol University, to act as chairman. Sir Philip accepted and the committee held its first meeting at the University on October 18th, 1946. Under the wise chairmanship of this brilliant man, the committee has been for the last ten years a model of management for every ambitious theatre company in the country.

When the company reopened in September 1946, Hugh Hunt had been able to redeem the pledge he had made at the inaugural meeting in the previous December. The reception accorded to the company in the first weeks of the opening season had convinced him that he was right in his belief that there was a public in Bristol for a three weeks' run of each play. Moreover, in practice, the members of the company greatly disliked having to pack up in their dressing-room at the end of the second week, and take the unpleasant nightly journey to play in another theatre, where their reception was never as cordial as in their home town. The visiting companies, although some of them had star artists, were also not as welcome as they might have been at the Theatre Royal— already a feeling was growing up among the theatregoers of Bristol: 'We want our own company; we don't want these strangers.' Encouraged by these signs, Hunt consulted with Cyril Wood, the regional director of the Arts Council in Bristol, and with other people prominent in the cultural life of the city. It was decided to try to form a club, an organised body of playgoers, who could be relied upon to give and encourage support for the company. A meeting was called for a Sunday in July 1946. It was a sweltering day, when it might have been anticipated that every reasonable person would be idling in his car or out on the neighbouring beaches. To the general amazement (except to that of Hunt, who had expected nothing else), a huge queue formed outside the theatre, and a crocodile stretched all along King Street. Every seat in the theatre was taken, and just as many people were turned away. Cyril Wood presided and it was decided then and there to form a 'Bristol Old Vic Club'. Membership of the club was not to bring with it any concession in the price of seats; the only advantage accruing would be the right to attend lectures and the feeling that the individual was helping to stimulate the interest in the premier theatre company of the West of England.

Over a thousand members were enrolled within the next fortnight. Cyril Wood became the first chairman, a position he filled with grace and tact for the next two years. After the club had been formed there was no doubt in anyone's mind that a three weeks' run for each play was possible. The new season in the autumn of 1946 set the pattern, and all plays have since run three weeks, sometimes extending to four weeks.

A further important step in Hunt's programme also came to fruition in the early autumn of 1946. This was the establishment of the Bristol Old Vic School, which was formally opened by Sir (then Mr.) Laurence Olivier on October 21st, 1946. Like all the other ventures at Bristol, this did not have an easy birth. Hunt had put the idea of a school both to the Governors of the Old Vic and to the Arts Council in the early summer, but it had not found great favour in either quarter. The Governors eventually agreed to it, but the Arts Council at first definitely vetoed it. They felt that the scheme, as put forward, was on too narrow a scale to be of any advantage to the prospective students. They themselves were already heavily committed to large-scale support of the ill-fated St. Denis School at the London Old Vic, so they did not feel tempted to encourage any other grandiose scheme at Bristol. Eventually, thanks once again to the wise guidance of Sir Ernest Pooley, the Council agreed to the establishment of the school, provided that its aim was to be self-supporting, and that the whole financial responsibility be undertaken by the Old Vic. At the same time they promised a modest annual guarantee of £250 against loss. And so the school was started in a single room over a greengrocer's store facing the theatre. The first director was Edward Stanley, who retained the position for eight years.   [C.L.]

The Importance of Being Earnest is always sure of its public, and in this sense Wilde's masterpiece was a safe choice to open Bristol's second Old Vic season on September 2nd, 1946. In other respects there were dangers: the definitive performances of Edith Evans and John Gielgud as Lady Bracknell and John Worthing have set a standard in period and comedy style difficult for later players to follow, and this is true even to an extent in the other parts: few who saw the modern London productions are likely to forget Gwen Ffrangcon-Davies's languorous Gwendolen Fairfax—needle-pointed under the eiderdown of society manners, a lovely but unmistakable chip off the maternal block; nor Peggy Ashcroft's dewy-rose Cicely with its lurking thorn of determination.

Wilde called his play 'a trivial comedy for serious people', which suggests the call for adult polish in the playing. The *Bristol Evening World* noted the repertory danger: 'such a brilliant piece of artificiality needs the most delicate touch—one slip and the glass cracks. It didn't crack many times last night, though the sheen was misty in places'. John Coe of the *Bristol Evening Post* thought Jane Henderson 'a first-class Lady Bracknell even though she was not quite rich or basso enough'; it is difficult to imagine this brilliant and stylish character actress failing with such congenial material. But it is equally difficult to see the sombre-faced and voiced William Devlin as John Worthing: too good an actor not to put up a creditable performance, he must have lacked the true bubble of wit or delicacy of touch. He 'tried hard to be a character when he should have tried to be elegant and characterless', wrote the critic of the *Western Daily Press*. Thomas Heathcote, who just before the war had been with the London Old Vic, appeared as Algernon with Everley Gregg, another fine character actress, as Miss Prism, and Kenneth Connor as the Rev. Chasuble. Ann Heffernan played Gwendolen and Joanna Horder Cicely. Hugh Hunt produced, with settings and costumes by Anthony Holland: and Hunt also spoke a special prologue to the season and play written once again by the indefatigable Christopher Hassall.

For *Tess*, the second play on October 2nd, Wendy Hiller joined the company, staying also for two further productions. A programme note welcomed the actress and at the same time expressed the reason for varying repertory teamwork with the introduction of such international stars. 'It is essential to provide the greatest variety of plays, and there comes a time when the casting of these plays, however carefully they are chosen, puts too great a strain on the flexibility of a small permanent body of actors. At such a moment the company benefits by extending its limits to embrace newcomers. The important condition in such invitations is that they are willing to join as members of our team.'

Tess of the D'Urbervilles, founded on Thomas Hardy's novel by the actress's husband Ronald Gow, was an admirable choice of part for Wendy Hiller in her Old Vic début. The heather and moors of the north which saw her birth are not vitally different in feeling from the countryside of Hardy's Wessex, and the candid strength of Wendy Hiller's approach to a character not alien to Tess. The clear-boned beauty of her face matched the part, and there was an elemental warmth and drive about her which moved naturally among the Druid columns of Stonehenge in the final scene of parting with Angel.

Gow began his play half-way through the book; a keen technical stroke that justified itself in stage performance, which concentrated on the culmination of Tess's tragedy (it is possible Ibsen would have adapted the story in this way). But the triumph was Wendy Hiller's ('Wendy Hiller Transcends All' was a typical Bristol headline), and it was no doubt the power of her performance that the following month drove the play to London, where it was performed at the New Theatre during the London Old Vic Company's visit to Paris. Jane Henderson as Mrs. Crumb, Everley Gregg as Mrs. Durbeyfield and Hilda Shroder as Tess's young sister were also outstanding, and Devlin sensitively pointed the difficult character of Angel, which psychologically fared worst in its transference from the book. ('Within the remote depths of his constitution, so gentle and affectionate as he was in general, there lay hidden a hard logical deposit, like a vein of metal in a soft loam, which turned the edge of everything that attempted to traverse it', wrote Hardy: a shrewd psychological analysis of the hard metal that destroyed Tess which became lost in the play, making Angel's rejection purely melodramatic.) Hunt again produced, with a décor by Guy Sheppard that painted, with vivid economy, the monolithic sunset of desolate Stonehenge.

In *Playboy of the Western World* on October 22nd, Wendy Hiller turned from Wessex to Ireland, and with coaching from Cyril Cusack produced a dependable Pegeen Mike, a country lass to her bone and without the inborn, long-forgotten family aristocracy of ill-starred Tess. But the triumph of this performance was Cyril Cusack's Playboy, Christy Mahon, already known to Oxford and London as well as Dublin.

'Miss Hiller', wrote John Garrett, 'tried conscientiously but she never was an adequate partner to the spontaneous and lyrical loveliness of Cyril Cusack's Playboy.' The *Western Daily Press* flowered into Synge pastiche: 'There's a man here called Cyril Cusack and shure it's the Cushat dove that the boy is and wasn't it Mr. Agate himself that said of the lad in O'Casey's *Plough and the Stars* that it was a blazing masterpiece, superbly acted, and isn't this just as good only he older an' more winsome with the pearls of the dawn flickering through the fog of peat-smoke about his borrowed breeches?' 'The word is—magnificent, flaming, magnificent.' And Gerard Fay in the *Manchester Guardian* took a breathtaking acting parallel: 'Mr. Hugh Hunt—a former producer at the Abbey Theatre in Dublin—has avoided all the dangers that beset anybody trying to present Synge to an English audience with a mainly English cast. . . . This brings us to the Playboy himself and the admission that the earlier part of this notice is slightly deceptive—as if one had said in a different context that some producer had made a brave shot at *Phèdre* in French with a mainly English cast except for one who happened to be Sarah Bernhardt. For the Christy Mahon is Cyril Cusack, who, in Dublin, has made the part peculiarly his own.'

Cusack's Christy is in fact a classic performance of our time—'our' in this case stretching from Dublin to London and Paris; for this actor who has Cockney as well as pure Irish in his veins (he is related to Dan Leno on the mother's side) has seen with genius that below Christy's arrogance and flights of imagination there lurk not only a poet but an inferiority complex in reverse, and through all the scintillations of his comedy there are felt the agonies of the frustrated and the hunted. The Christy who suddenly turns and flashes defiance at his tormentors is the Christy of his own imagination, born in this moment of hunted rebellion but always below the surface of his boasting and uncertainty; and the actor's subtle realisation of this was the key to the emotional, as well as comic, impact of his performance: tender and sharp like a damson from the wood, a Leprechaun with a hint of the Dickens sparrow the actor can also play so well.

Hugh Hunt, a former producer of the Abbey Theatre, of which Cusack was a member at this time, produced the play, with settings designed by Guy Sheppard and painted by Daphne Lord. 'It has atmosphere and, by way of a fire burning in the open hearth, it goes so far that it even has the correct smoky smell of an Irish cottage', wrote John Bennett. Jane Henderson's 'virago of a Widow Quinn' was admired, and Hunt again stepped in for an absent actor when Devlin, who played Pegeen's father, took a night off on October 29th to see Olivier's Lear in London.

On November 17th, as a stepping-stone to his own Lear, Devlin played Shylock in *The Merchant of Venice*.

'Shylock needs something more than craftsmanship, and that something Mr. Devlin has', wrote the *Western Daily Press*. 'Is it intellectual integrity? Is it a capacity for suffering? Whatever it may be this is an enormously human Shylock. . . . Seeing this Shylock we see and understand both the proprietor of an East End "sweat shop" and the fanatical leader of Fighting Zion. Moreover, we do not harden against him. . . . We identify his cause even if we do not follow it. There is the Jew tragedy about him but there is more, there is the tragedy of the materialist of any race. And it becomes, so powerful is the picture, an indictment not only of the evil in man, but in mankind. This Shylock is the mirror to ourselves.' It was, he summed up, 'a great Shylock', and Dennis Bushell concurred: 'a Shylock that is a little restless, perhaps, and apt to pose, but nevertheless a great one'.

Devlin's performance was the main distinction of a production by Stuart Latham much trounced for its incidental music by Christian Darnton, which was allowed moreover to intrude on the text. 'Why, above all', snarled Garrett, 'was the production nearly wrecked on the rocks of the most irrelevant and impertinent "music" that I have yet heard in any theatre?' These 'sepulchral noises from the orchestra pit' damped the spirit of carnival, and the costumes of Berkeley Sutcliffe were felt by some of the actresses to be too fanciful and fussy. Wendy Hiller as a Shakespearian actress was also considered by one critic to be 'in the early morning of her talent . . . the Portia of a schoolgirl, fresh and irresponsible'. But Garrett was enchanted. 'Her turning away from Bassanio on the line, "Beshrew your eyes, They have o'er lookt me, and divided me" was a gesture of inspired insight. Her joy at his right choice was conveyed with such unaffected sincerity that I found it more moving than anything throughout *Tess*.'

Rosalie Crutchley, another leading player from the Oxford Repertory (where she had been Pegeen Mike to Cusack's Playboy) and from Gielgud's wartime repertory season at the Haymarket Theatre, joined the company to play a 'smouldering Jessica', with Manning Wilson as Antonio, Geoffrey Edwards as Bassanio, Norman Claridge as Morocco, Kathleen Hilditch as Nerissa and Stuart Burge as Launcelot Gobbo. While Devlin and Wendy Hiller played in *Tess* in London, their parts were taken over by Stuart Latham, the producer, and Meriel Moore.

J. B. Priestley's new play, *An Inspector Calls*, was produced at Bristol on December 10th, 1946, while it was still in the repertoire of the London Old Vic Company at the New Theatre, where it had received its first production on October 1st. It was a triumph for Rosalie Crutchley as Sheila Birling, 'darkly crystalline in its beauty', a black pearl after the elegant white diamond of Margaret Leighton's performance in London. It was, wrote Garrett, 'a firm and fine piece of acting. The character grew and developed as the impact of events took its toll. She brought sensitiveness and understanding to the part, and her line, "And it's just the wrong time not to believe me", was most movingly spoken'.

But this play of responsibility for a suicide who never appears, coincidental but symbolic of society's capability of developing a conscience too late, was altogether a major achievement of the Bristol Old Vic to date. It was, affirmed the *Western Daily Press*, 'Hugh Hunt's best production ever in Bristol, with the best-balanced and most perfect teamwork of a cast we have seen for ten or fifteen years. . . . The atmosphere at two performances we attended was uncanny. We had the impression that the actors were in some way oblivious of the audience and were gripped so powerfully in this beautifully phrased play that they were enwrapt in their parts to a most unusual extent'.

Devlin's Inspector—the *deus ex machina* of the action—ranked too among his firmest and most sympathetic performances: it was 'finely controlled with very great understanding'. Norman Claridge and Meriel Moore as Mr. and Mrs. Birling, Kenneth Connor as Eric Birling, John Bailey as Gerald Croft and Philippa Sparrow as Edna completed the small cast. As in London, the settings and 1912 costumes were designed by Kathleen Ankers.

J. B. Fagan's adaptation of *Treasure Island* was the Christmas attraction, and an obvious success which enabled Devlin to have macabre fun with Long John Silver while preparing for the stupendous task of King Lear.

The challenging Shakespearian tragedy of *King Lear*, on January 22nd, 1947, was the first anniversary production of the Bristol Old Vic (it was also to be the tenth). Hunt had produced Devlin's first Lear, at the Westminster Theatre, in 1934, when the twenty-two-year-old actor had made a shattering impact, following

47

it with another Lear, under Henry Cass at the Old Vic, two years later. It has not greatly developed with the years, a certain inflexibility of voice being its main defect; its power exceeds its pathos, though the noble Blakean head and impressive presence (for in spite of his small height this actor can suggest physical dominance) make for a striking total impression, with a tone of bronze that burns with sombre splendour through the flash and fury of the storm. He assumed, wrote *The Times* when the production moved to the Embassy Theatre in London during May, 'what is virtually a convention for tragedy: the noble mask, the large and limited rhetorical gestures, the superficial heroic generalisation, so to speak, in place of what must be first human and particular'.

Bristol was loyal and less inclined to seek flaws in this monolithic statuary. 'This is a great Lear from a character actor who ranks with the first two or three in England . . . enormous and powerful majesty.' For Garrett 'He was always miles removed from senility. He was huge in the sweep of his moral grandeur'.

The cast was altogether a fine one. Rosalie Crutchley's Goneril, wrote Coe, 'must rank with the greatest of Gonerils'. 'Like a red incestuous snake' was the *Western Daily Press* description. 'She flames and burns. She creates also a clear and precise relationship with all she touches; particularly Mr. Robert Eddison's cold unpleasantness as Edmund.' With Meriel Moore as Regan and the small but talented Hilda Shroder as Cordelia, 'the trio of daughters', wrote Philip Hope-Wallace, 'are a good example of how talent in acting and production may happily combine. It is long since one saw each character so well defined, plausibly drawn, and effectively "growing" '.

Unfortunately, two of the most outstanding performances, those of Robert Eddison as Edmund and Leon Quartermaine as Kent, did not reach London: a severe loss in both cases, for Eddison, unexpectedly in an actor who has excelled as Prospero and the Archangel Raphael, drove vividly into the Renaissance evil of Edmund, and Quartermaine's Kent, with its voice of gold-threaded silk, was incomparable in loyalty and tenderness of devotion ('Here we are on the high Alps of the theatre', commented the *Western Daily Press*, and Alan Dent wrote, 'I have never before seen Kent's terrible grief at the old king's failure to recognise him so movingly conveyed'). Kenneth Connor as the Fool was also much

admired, and gained tribute from several who admitted they still
had Alec Guinness's superb Fool of the London Old Vic *Lear*
vividly in mind.

With settings of reddened and thundery skies by Guy Sheppard,
Hugh Hunt's production did its best, in limited space, to catch
the impact of the play. 'The grouping of the final scene', wrote
Dent, 'makes one of the most beautiful stage-pictures I have ever
beheld—Goneril and Regan picturesquely dead on their thrones
on one side, Edmund picturesquely dead on the other, and everybody else left alive circling round Lear in his last anguish over the
dead Cordelia.'

On April 19th the company turned to the lighter monarchy
of Shaw's *The Apple Cart*: a 'political extravaganza' of a Labour
ministry that has not lost its wit and point with the years. It was
produced by Stuart Latham with Manning Wilson as King
Magnus, Norman Claridge as Boanerges, Meriel Moore as the
Queen and Elizabeth Gray as Orinthia. Kenneth Connor's United
States Ambassador, who makes so devastating an appearance in
the last act with his offer of American return to the British
Commonwealth, won special praise.

A new play, Vivian Connell's *Throng O' Scarlet*, followed the
Shaw, with Margaretta Scott joining the company for a leading
part. Its impact was savage, literate and artistically schizophrenic.
A play set in the hunting world, the scarlet of its coats had the
violence of a blood-bath. 'When Mr. Vivian Connell grows out of
the violence that is in him', wrote the *Western Daily Press*, 'he
will handle his characters, all of them, as though he loves them.
At the moment he hates. The fire burns him up. The blaze of his
Irish wrath stirs up the stench of hatred as surely as he stirs up the
stench of dead horses stewing in the slaughterhouse in this play
of the hunting people of Cloneen. . . . A mad Irishman? Certainly.
But the poetry is in him and this play is worth a hundred of your
milk-and-water card-index blatherings because it is written at
white heat.' W. A. Darlington, in the *Daily Telegraph*, also
referred to the 'vigorous and imaginative writing', and added
the author 'lacks the ability to tell a clear story, and allows our
interest in his characters to dissipate itself in consequence'. The
atmosphere, according to Lionel Hale, was of 'Irish hunting folk
as seen by some highly excitable Celtic Tchehov. . . . I do not
recall ever seeing so brilliantly written a bad play'. And *The Times*

clinched the artistic bewilderment: 'The combination of skilful production, vigorous racy dialogue, good acting, and an extraordinarily bad play is disconcerting.'

Kenneth Connor had as Mikey what is recalled now as 'the most gentle and moving part he ever played', and one of the minor eccentric memories of the run of this play (in addition to the author's demand for a real dead horse in the second act) is of this actor in full costume taking one of the hounds of the Beaufort Pack for his nightly jaunt 'round the block' outside the theatre. Devlin's tortured Master of the Hunt, Harry Boyle, is also remembered from the long cast. 'The cast were all caught up in the play's magic', wrote a behind-scenes worker later, 'and Connor's long speech on the blood and dirt and splendour of the hunt is still there, somewhere—echoing round the empty stage—at night.' Hugh Hunt produced, with settings by Frederick Crooke.

Controversy raged among the audience and in the press, and was hardly stilled by Hunt's next production of *Much Ado About Nothing* in modern dress. With *King Lear*, this was later played in London. The Bristol headlines were illustrative of the treatment: 'Wardens to the Rescue!'—'Shakespeare Comes to Town—On a Push-Bike!' The atmosphere actually was of Italy under arms, not totally inappropriate to the Shakespeare atmosphere of an army returning to women and celebration. 'The curtain goes up on the courtyard of an Italian mansion', wrote the *Western Daily Press*, 'the shadows of peach trees fall on a sunlit wall, vines hang in the silent air and the deep blue Italian night is lit with stars. Three girls sit beneath a tree, whispering over their needlework. In a corner two old men bend over a chess-board. This scene is timeless. . . .' To much of this Kathleen Ankers's setting contributed. 'The statuary has that air of accidental loveliness which captivates the eye in Italy', wrote Garrett. 'Miss Ankers has exactly caught what was wanted, whether on the porch or in the flying cherubim over the chapel's altar. The brooding figure of the Virgin in the background served to remind us that the antics of these humans were indeed much ado about nothing, and that in very fact "our little life is rounded with a sleep".'

Dogberry on a bicycle, in a siren suit with A.R.P. headgear, was a key to the comedy. In London the critics were more divided, half finding the production exciting and the rest feeling only irritated. The actors inevitably tended to take second place, and Rosalie Crutchley, whose dark eyes and sculptured cheek-bones reflect a thundery rather than sunny personality, never felt entirely at her ease in the Elizabethan repartee of Beatrice. 'She is', wrote *The Times*, 'inclined to glower. But give her a passage of words with Benedick, and she is charming, and in the church scene and after she is moved.'

Clement McCallin, an Anglo-American actor who had been a pre-war Henry V at Stratford-on-Avon, played Benedick (and also Edmund in London), with 'so much attack and pace that I feared he might be consumed by his own vitality', remarked John Coe. He is a forceful and attractive if not subtle actor. Devlin, un-expectedly, was the Dogberry, with Manning Wilson as Don John, Claridge as Don Pedro and Hilda Shroder as Hero. [A.W.]

CHAPTER FOUR

The Third Season
1947 *to* 1948

BEFORE THE SEASON OPENED in the autumn of 1947 there had been important changes in the Arts Council, which affected the working of the Bristol Old Vic Company. In the spring of that year, Michael MacOwan had resigned as drama director, and his place had been taken by Llewellyn Rees, who had formerly been general secretary of the British Actors' Equity Association. MacOwan was a producer and Rees was an executive officer, and the different approach, as it affected the company, might be described as an emphasis on finance, rather than an emphasis on artistic prowess—or more correctly as an attempt to mould artistic achievement within the possibilities of finance. There had been two productions during the 1946-7 season which had been extremely successful both artistically and in their drawing power—*King Lear* and *Treasure Island*—yet both had lost money. An examination of their budgets showed that even if there had not been an empty seat at any performance these productions would still not have covered their expenses. In the case of *King Lear* there was the excuse that negotiations had taken place between Hugh Hunt and the British Council, and the prospect had been envisaged that *King Lear* might be taken on an extended tour of the Continent; and that, therefore, any money lost on the production at Bristol would be recouped. For *Treasure Island* there was no such excuse; the simple truth was that no efforts or money had been spared in the desire to give Bristol a superb Christmas production.

It was Llewellyn Rees and Sir Philip Morris who saw that such a mistaken attitude of the 'Arts Council will pay' could not be maintained, and from that moment forward Hugh Hunt's productions had a different orientation. The scenery was more simple and less realistic, the plays had smaller casts. Making a virtue out of necessity the productions developed a new and typically 'Bristol' style. The immediate result was that for the first time the accounts of the company showed a profit. The balance sheet for the year 1947-8 (which did not absolutely coincide with the season but was from March to March) was £1,800 on the right side for the company, with another £2,800 in profits from bars and programmes, or £4,600 in all—a remarkable transition from the net loss of about £4,000 in the previous year.

The third season saw the beginning of an ambitious movement, which for a time held out great promise. This was the South-West Association of Theatre Companies, the root idea of which came from the Drama Department of the Arts Council. (A brief note about the scheme in *The Times* evoked the annoyance of the Council, because no one in the Drama Department had bothered to tell them anything about it.)

Put shortly, the idea was a collaboration between the five repertory companies in the South-West of England, with the Bristol company in the role of the elder brother. The other companies involved were the Salisbury Arts Theatre Company, the West of England Theatre Company based on Exmouth, the Avon Players from Falmouth, and the English Ring Actors from Penzance. Though everyone realised that life in the theatre would never develop according to rule and rote, the basic plan was that of the 'ladder' system. Students from the Bristol school should go to the four smaller companies, the leading artists should move up yearly to Bristol, leading artists from Bristol should play as occasional 'guests' in the smaller towns. A preliminary conference was held at Bristol in December 1947, and in the spring of 1948 a production course for producers, stage directors and scene designers was held at Bristol under the supervision of Hugh Hunt and Edward Stanley, the principal of the school. A number of distinguished lecturers came from London, including Michel St. Denis from the Old Vic school; the 'students' sat in on Hunt's rehearsals of *Hamlet*, and they paid visits to a number of theatres, including the Salisbury Arts Theatre, and the Little Theatre in Bristol, where they were the guests of Ronald Russell, that distinct and outspoken personality, who for over a quarter of a century has gaily kept the flag of repertory flying in the West of England.

Allan Davis had been appointed assistant director of the Bristol Old Vic Company at the beginning of the 1947-8 season, and this gave Hugh Hunt more leisure for administrative work. Hunt went round the various companies from Penzance to Salisbury,

criticising and appraising, and he took active steps in the furtherance of the basic plan. Artists from Falmouth, Exmouth and
Salisbury were invited to Bristol to play smaller parts in *Hamlet*
and *The Second Mrs. Tanqueray*, on the explicit understanding
that at the end of their engagements they would return to their
original companies. The stage seemed set for an impressive movement which might have had far-reaching effects upon the whole
repertory movement of the country. Unfortunately, within a year
or two, two of the companies—Falmouth and Penzance—ceased
to exist, and after Hunt's departure to London in the spring of
1949 the driving force behind the plan faded out, and the scheme
has never been revived. The West of England Theatre Company,
under the influence of its energetic director, Joyce Worsley, is
still, however, in close touch with Bristol, and every year Mrs.
Worsley takes two or three students from the Bristol school.
Phyllida Law is among the young people who have done their
gruelling year with this company, touring each play for three
weeks, in the course of which time they visit about eleven towns.
A hard but vivifying experience for the young artist.   [C.L.]

'There has never been another season like that and never will
be', wrote a former Bristol Old Vic student and paint-dock worker
to the author of *Paul Rogers* after its publication in 1956; and this
opinion of this historic season under Hunt which now started
seems widely shared to this day by the regular audience, as well
as by some actors who remember it. Catherine Lacey and Robert
Eddison joined Devlin to lead the company, and were already
established players who were now to do some of their finest and
widest range of work (Rogers is only one of their colleagues to
continue to sing their praises and regret London playgoers never
had a chance to judge the remarkable versatility of their work at
Bristol). And although Rogers himself was unknown to begin
with—a young actor who had just played for six months at the
Colchester Repertory after six years in the Royal Navy—he
quickly made an impression as a character actor of outstanding
gifts, and garnered a loyal public of his own. Elizabeth Sellars
and Jane Wenham, young actresses of future quality, also joined
the team.

Continuing the tradition of a Wilde opening to the season,
An Ideal Husband was staged on September 1st, 1947: not without

unexpected publicity, for Elizabeth Sellars broke into the headlines by receiving a black eye when attacked on her way to a London rehearsal, and the first-night scenes at the theatre were broadcast by the B.B.C.

'Against a background of rustling silk and the clash of malicious wit, Wilde's epigrams fell from Mr. Eddison's lips with an ease and charm that will win him many admirers', wrote John Coe. His Viscount Goring was in fact a perfect piece of casting and a model of comedy style, admirably bolstered by Catherine Lacey's poise and attack. 'She brought a full armoury of talents to the playing of Mrs. Cheveley, and evoked all Vienna in her person', according to John Garrett. William Devlin's Sir Robert Chiltern, a duller part, understandably evoked less praise (two critics became aware of some mannerisms creeping into his work, and a lack of range of gesture), but Elizabeth Sellars's beauty and poise irradiated the Edwardian grace of Lady Chiltern. Jane Wenham played the minor part of Mabel Chiltern, with Paul Rogers, thirty years old, making an initial success as the ancient and bewhiskered Earl of Caversham, of (judging by the photographs) a cavernous yawn.

Anthony Holland's settings were particularly admired for their richness and sense of period: he was a young designer who had just achieved the distinction of having decorated four plays running simultaneously in the West End. Hunt produced with his usual polish.

Priestley's *The Linden Tree*, which followed on September 23rd, was well adapted to the company and in some cases was better cast than in the West End. In spite of Sybil Thorndike's wonderfully moving performance at the Duchess Theatre, many felt Catherine Lacey's Mrs. Linden the more credible performance—its being just conceivable that this woman would be capable, at the end, of the selfishness of breaking the lifelong tie with the professor, her husband, and making a new life away from the hated provincial university—a situation never quite conceivable in Sybil Thorndike's personality and an apparent weakness of the play in town. Eddison, too, gave an intensely real psychological interpretation of the spiv-like son Rex, Elizabeth Sellars was firmly believable as the French Catholic daughter, and Jane Wenham an enchanting teenager as the music-loving youngest child, Dinah. Devlin played Professor Linden in a carefully realistic make-up;

55

another deeply felt and sympathetic performance. The teamwork more than justified Priestley's recent declaration that 'here in Bristol is a body of artists who are the equal of the majority to be found in London's West End'.

The third production, *Othello*, on October 14th, was also produced by Hugh Hunt, with settings by Alan Barlow. Devlin once again clutched at the peaks of Shakespearian tragedy, and missed to an extent by his literal lack of inches. His Othello, wrote the *Western Daily Press* in an admirably detailed notice, 'begins quietly. The command "Keep up your bright swords" comes with no flash, the speech to the Senate is delivered with fine negroid resonance, but with the African fire well dampened, "Hold, for your lives" is lost in the general hubbub and the dreadful bell is ordered to be silenced in tones which suggest that the man tolling does not need to be told. He holds his fire until we see the whites of his eyes. Everything is held in reserve for the outburst of disillusion.

'The result is that something is lost of nobility early on, but the expression of temperament gains force. Mr. Devlin's Moor cannot by nature be a magnificent animal to the eye, but to the ear he becomes a rippling savage. His passion is a primitive strumming of the vocal chords. Physically, he strives to move us, never quite succeeding in direct proportion to the sweat of his brow. But vocally it is a great performance.'

Garrett, too, blended admiration with dissatisfaction. 'Too often his grief was Shylock's and not Othello's. He pathetically stooped and bit the dust in misery when he should surely have thrown back his shoulders and taken it as the great soldier he was.'

It was Devlin's last performance as a regular member of the Bristol Old Vic Company; if not his greatest triumph, still a performance of stature (in the metaphorical sense) and passionate sonority.

Eddison's Iago was generally accounted outstanding: '. . . quite the best I have ever seen—the handsomest, the wittiest, the most radiantly "honest" and the first in my experience to do the right thing in all those all-important soliloquies. That is, suddenly to remove his mask of likeableness (which for so long takes in even his own wife) and let his ambitions shoot up burningly, like an evil flame.' This *News Chronicle* verdict was upheld in Bristol: 'can rank with any Iago to be seen today', wrote the *Western Daily Press*.

The Playboy of the Western World (Synge), 1946. Cyril Cusack as
Christy Mahon and Wendy Hiller as Pegeen Mike.

Desmond Tripp

Much Ado About Nothing, 1947. Rosalie Crutchley as Beatrice and
Clement McCallin as Benedick.

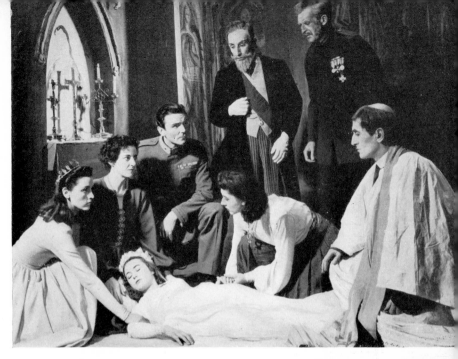

ABOVE: *Much Ado About Nothing*, 1947. Church scene. Modern dress production by Hugh Hunt. L. *to* R. Rosalie Crutchley (Beatrice), Meriel Moore, Hilda Shroder (Hero), Clement McCallin (Benedick), Bettine Milne, Marne Maitland, Norman Claridge and Edward Stanley (Friar Francis).

BELOW: *Much Ado About Nothing*, 1954. Church scene. Production by John Moody. L. *to* R. Edward Hardwicke (Friar Francis), Edgar Wreford Benedick),) Perlita Neilson (Hero) and Rosemary Harris (Beatrice).

Both photos by Desmond Tripp

King Lear, 1947. William Devlin as Lear and Leon
Quartermaine as Kent.

But there is no doubt the triumph of the play was the youthful Jane Wenham's Desdemona, Garrett only feeling she lacked 'tragic stature' till her Willow Scene of 'agonising intensity'. 'Tender and affecting'—'played with a touching sincerity and an ethereal quality': such Bristol praise was clinched by Harold Conway's enthusiasm in the London *Evening Standard*: 'It is in the highways and by-ways of theatreland that the West End stars of the future are often to be found. . . . There is a nineteen-year-old girl named Jane Wenham playing with the Bristol Old Vic Company. In a most interesting production of *Othello*, her Desdemona is the finest I have seen since Peggy Ashcroft appeared with Paul Robeson. . . . If she continues her work in Bristol at her Desdemona level, I shall expect to see her in London next year as a star.'

The Cassio was felt to be colourless, and Rogers's Roderigo —well flaxed upon the distaff—too Aguecheek-like; but Catherine Lacey made an inevitably fine thing of Emilia, and the production, aglow with colour, was praised by Coe for its 'unerring pictorial groupings'.

On November 4th Bristol gave the first performance of Peter Watling's *Rain on the Just*, a play later produced in London with Marie Ney and Michael Denison in the leading parts. It was a play apposite to today, with its aristocratic families in decline, trying desperately to keep the historical family mansion from passing into alien hands, or like the witty, selfish and wholly realist elder son, Sir Nicolas Corbel, of this play, urging its sale and the elimination of an estate which can only be retained by constant sacrifice.

It is only after the rather tentative first act that Watling gets to serious grips with his theme, which he slightly hampers by the introduction of a more novelettish small drama of the marriage of the younger son to a Nurse, who (surprisingly, in view of her profession) becomes hysterical under the influence of claustro-phobic tradition in the house. But as a television production recently showed, the latter part of the play has quality and the character of the dominating mother, ready to sacrifice everything to retain the family inheritance, is well drawn. Catherine Lacey at Bristol played her remarkably, drawing a real lady perfectly in type and unmistakable beneath the shapeless garden hat and worn-out cardigan (incorrectly buttoned) of her first entrance; inflexible of will, tragic in a losing fight, an aristocrat to her nervous fingertips.

Robert Eddison's Sir Nicolas was also a performance as rich in character as in humour: 'Robert Eddison', wrote J. C. Trewin in *The Observer*, 'points the argument sharply: he speaks poignards. This edged, poised performance is the triumph of a play, civilised, dramatic—but with few run-of-the-mill theatrics—that should have in time a metropolitan audience and a larger (though no more beautiful) home than the green-and-gold casket of Bristol's Theatre Royal.' There was a brilliant characterisation by Pauline Winter— which the actress later repeated in London and on television— of the dowdy, half-wit daughter. Rachel Gurney joined the company as Nicolas's fiancée, with Elizabeth Sellars as the Nurse and Paul Rogers as the family butler, Troke. Hunt produced with a setting by Margaret Tracey.

Great Expectations, in the adaptation by Alec Guinness, brought an outstanding Dickensian portrait by Paul Rogers as Joe Gargery. Catherine Lacey again shone as the eccentric Miss Havisham, with Jane Wenham in the difficult part of her ruthless but enchanting young protégée, Estella. Eddison was the Pip, Alexander Gauge a 'sweet' Mr. Pumblechook (the epithet is Rogers's) and Rolf Lefebvre a brilliant Dickensian Mr. Jaggers. Ernest Hare, long known at the London Old Vic, played the convict, Elizabeth Sellars the tranquil Biddy, and Joseph James the cast-iron comedy role of Herbert Pocket ('looking around') which Guinness himself had chosen to act so engagingly in town.

Aladdin, the Clinton-Baddeley—Walter Leigh pantomime, followed Dickens as a Christmas attraction, and registered Paul Rogers's first resounding triumph with the company. His Widow Twankey took the stage in a manner so authentic that many who had not recently followed the fortunes of the Theatre Royal believed him to have been specially imported for the pantomime. 'A more gorgeously comic Widow than any recent Dame we can remember', wrote John Coe, and the actor was freely compared with George Lacey, who had made his début as a Dame on the same Theatre Royal stage.

Eddison also effected a feminine transformation as the Empress of China, and Nuna Davey, later a stalwart of the Bristol company and of the Players' Theatre pantomimes, was the robust Fairy Dew-Drop, in full ballet tutu, who enchanted the adults as naughtily satirical while the children, equally entranced, accepted her as the beautiful reality. Marie Burke was the Principal Boy, and Allan Davis, Hunt's assistant, produced with designs by Terence Morgan II (a device adopted by the designer to distinguish him from the actor of the same name).

From the ridiculous to the sublime, in other words from pantomime China to Shakespearian Elsinore. *Hamlet* on February 3rd, 1948, marked Robert Eddison's début as the Prince and the whole production later in the year was transported to the St. James's Theatre in London, as Bristol's offering in the season of provincial repertory companies presented by Basil Dean.

Hunt's blending of the monolithic with rich tapestried backgrounds, and his use of lighting, attracted some attention, but interest inevitably centred on Hamlet, and Eddison's study, hampered a little by a rather feminine décolleté neckline, was received with respect and admiration tinctured with disagreement. 'A thoughtful, rich study, best in its quiet moments and its grim humour . . . a Hamlet driven in upon himself', wrote John Bennett. W. A. Darlington, later in London, regretted a certain 'softness and febrility' which prevented his becoming a figure of high tragedy: 'Hamlet is, and must be, a man. Mr. Eddison makes him an excitable boy'; and *The Times* as often was balanced and explicit:

> Mr. Robert Eddison in *Hamlet* is a compass in a magnetic storm. He points in all directions at once, and—emotionally— we scarcely know where we are.
>
> There is no gainsaying that the character has set the actor's imagination on fire. To all its challenges he responds, and responds with the utmost intelligence. . . . The points are made, but all too lightly; they are never driven home.

The critic sensed a 'moving among shadows', an 'unreality', in the portrait.

Harold Hobson, always an admirer of Eddison, was vivid in appreciation:

> I do not remember hearing the 'To be or not to be' soliloquy better delivered. Moving forward on an empty stage, taking full advantage of his great height, looking upward as if he would question the very skies, Mr. Eddison spoke it like a man

59

whose brain might crack under the strain imposed by its metaphysical conundrums.

I have never seen a more restless Hamlet. He is restless not because he is ill at ease, but because inside his skull are seven devils.

Hamlet is an extraordinarily difficult test for the actor, because each critic already carries in his own mind some very strong and personal expectations as to interpretation; the winds of criticism blow the actor in all directions, and few escape unscathed. Eddison's performance rode the storm, if not unscathed, at least with intelligence and talent unquestioned, and like Michael Redgrave, whose first Hamlet also occurred at the age of forty or thereabouts, his suggestion of a young prince was easily achieved.

Catherine Lacey was perforce a Gertrude of more than average brain (many felt her miscast), Alexander Gauge a 'bloat' Claudius and Paul Rogers a Polonius, wrote Ivor Brown, 'like a piece of the Stone Age walking'. Jane Wenham's mad scene as Ophelia was specially praised, but none of the other acting was notable. In the St. James's Theatre production in July a future Bristol leading actor, Edgar Wreford, made his stage début among the anonymous courtiers.

On March 2nd Pinero followed Shakespeare, and *The Second Mrs. Tanqueray, Hamlet*. As Paula once again Catherine Lacey came into her own. 'Maurice Baring found seeing Duse as Mrs. Tanqueray an unforgettable emotional experience, and it is easy to see why', wrote Garrett. 'Miss Lacey had not understudied Mrs. Patrick Campbell in the part for nothing, and she played this riot of emotion up and down the scale with triumphant confidence. Even at the end one felt that she had still more tricks up her elegant sleeve. Whether she was impish, wheedling, mischievous or viperish, she rang the bell every time. Her range of tone never failed her. She brought to the part pose and repose, passion, pathos, excitement, mystery, and imagination . . . a great piece of bravura in the grand tradition of English acting.'

It was the general verdict, from both outside and within the theatre, and inevitably other players were overshadowed, although Eddison, not quite rightly cast, had fun with Cayley Drummond (played with grey hair and a lisp), and Godfrey Kenton as Aubrey Tanqueray, Jane Wenham as Ellean and Paul Rogers as Sir

George Orreyed ('a model drunk') gave admirable support. Hunt's production was a stylish period piece with lavish settings and costumes by Alan Barlow.

James Bridie's *Tobias and the Angel*, on March 23rd, gave Rogers a chance at last to play his own age (in fact, younger), and many (including Garrett and the happy actor) thought this his most enchanting part and performance yet. This innocent abroad was, wrote a critic, 'delightfully done . . . never a line of comedy wasted', and there was reference to 'little gems of by-play' as well as the actor's perfect timing and charm. The naïveté of the character was beautifully contrasted with Eddison's Archangel Raphael, a part created by Henry Ainley and here given equal nobility of presence and of voice. 'Full of authority and power', wrote John Coe: a performance that seemed outlined in light.

Henry Manning shone for the first time in the company in the lovely part of blind Tobit, with Nuna Davey as Anna, his wife, and the beautiful Elizabeth Sellars as the rather equivocally-drawn Sara. As Sherah, a singing girl, Jane Wenham had a further opportunity to reveal the sweet soprano voice which had first been discovered in *Aladdin*. Allan Davis produced a series of 'lovely stage pictures', designed by Alix Stone. The incidental music was by John Dalby.

The Apple Orchards of the Soviet dramatist Leonid Leonof (who had won the Stalin Prize in 1942 for his play *Invasion*) brought an English stage première on April 13th, although the play had received a public reading a few years before in London with some famous players among the cast. The Moscow Arts Theatre gave its co-operation by providing photographs of the Russian production for study, as well as details of the stage instructions and gramophone recordings of Russian songs and dances. This offset to an extent Hugh Hunt's disappointment at official refusal to allow him to go to Moscow as planned, to discuss the play and suggested alterations with the author.

Hunt's producer's note in the programme suggests:

> The background of the characters is perhaps difficult for us to grasp.
>
> The Makkaveyef family lived in their present house before the 1914-18 war. Adrian, the father, fought in the war and after the revolution was made director of the State Apple Orchards.

His children are typical products of the revolution; keenly jealous of their country's honour and creed. Matvey Pwilyayef is the only person in the play who represents the political and social misfit. Although he once fought bravely as a partisan against the Germans, his courage failed him when he was arrested by them and he chose life with dishonour. Although the exact nature of his activities is not revealed to the family until the end of the play, his general attitude and 'return from the dead' arouse their instinctive suspicions.

It was a play of a large Russian family, the product of two marriages of the paterfamilias, Adrian Zimofeyevich Makkeveyef, the Director of a State Fruit Farm, and the Tchehovian charm was not absent. 'All the people within it, whatever their ages', observed *The Times*, 'see each other and themselves with the ardent curiosity of youth, and they are quite Tchehovian in their awareness of the soul and earth—up to a point—in the perception of life as a tragi-comedy. The point at which this perception is suddenly switched off is where family affairs entwine themselves with affairs of State. . . . Mr. Hugh Hunt has found for this difficult play a rhythm which gives all the tragi-comedy elements their proper force.'

It was, in fact, a good play which stirred the company to give of their best: years later one of the cast, Paul Rogers, still remembered it as a fine play in which Robert Eddison had given an outstanding performance as the old father ('Robert Eddison with Rasputin countenance and Chaliapin resonance presides over the family with authority', confirms the *Western Daily Press*). Rogers himself also achieved a remarkable characterisation of the 'misfit' Matvey. 'Here is a performance of extraordinary brilliance—the shuffling, half-remorseful, part-sadistic traitor', wrote John Bennett, and T. C. Kemp of the *Birmingham Post* concurred. Hunt himself thought it was Rogers's finest performance at Bristol.

Allan Cuthbertson joined the company to play the doctor son, Yury, of the first marriage, and Donald Sinden also made his first appearance with the Bristol Old Vic in the small part of a Red Navy officer. Catherine Lacey demonstrated her versatility as a little mousy schoolmistress (she was already rehearsing *Hedda Gabler*).

Hedda Gabler, produced by Allan Davis on May 4th, provided the actress with the now-expected triumph. 'It is the performance of her career', wrote Alan Dent, who added characteristically that it 'looks remarkably like Holbein's great portrait of the Duchess of Milan with the resigned and yet insinuating hands.' Coe 'watched her mesmerised' and Dennis Bushell ran to zoological metaphors: 'a sleek leopardess in *Tanqueray*, she is a tigress in this, now purring, now snarling, padding restlessly in a well-upholstered cage reeking of lavender and roseleaves'. 'Magnificent —a compelling study of the unbalanced mind', summed up the *Western Daily Press*.

Surprisingly, in the circumstances, other characters emerged well too: Coe praised the 'spinelessness and academic preoccupation' of Rolf Lefebvre's Tesman, and Dent admired Eddison's Eilert Lovborg, 'an infatuated soak none the worse, in his way, for looking like R. L. Stevenson'. Rogers as Judge Brack—with greying red hair, a beard and eyeglass—the *Western Daily Press* thought 'suave and menacing' ('rather like a slug' was the actor's own more pungent description). Meriel Moore returned to play the frightened but victorious Mrs. Elvsted, with Nuna Davey, rising in versatility, as the fluttering elderly aunt.

In *You Never Can Tell*, the last play of the season, Rogers had his first flop, though he was fortunately to return to retrieve it. His William the Waiter, 'with sniff and sidewhiskers' and 'not helped by an unfortunate make-up', depressed the actor no less than his principal critic (and normal admirer), Ivor Brown. But this early Shaw comedy always seems to go gaily in repertory, and with Eddison as Valentine, Jane Wenham as the prettiest of twins, Elizabeth Sellars as Gloria, Catherine Lacey as Mrs. Clandon and William Devlin as Bohun, Q.C., the stage was set for what Coe described as 'charm and boisterous fun'. 'Robert Eddison and Donald Sinden, as Valentine and Philip, are so good as to make us sigh that they weren't around when Jack and Algy were due to occupy the stage', wrote the *Western Daily Press*, and Ivor Brown, referring to 'two brilliant performances' by Catherine Lacey and Robert Eddison, added that 'Eddison's mixture of infatuation and apprehension, nerves and mischief, were beautifully portrayed in every moving of a roving eye and quivering lip'. Hunt produced, with sets by Margaret Tracey and costumes by Allan Barlow. [A.W.]

CHAPTER FIVE

The Fourth Season
1948 *to* 1949

THE FOURTH SEASON, which opened in September 1948, was to be Hugh Hunt's last season in Bristol. This is not the place to enlarge upon the internal quarrels and dissensions that were splitting the administration of the Old Vic in London, bickering which was to last for five years until a clean sweep of all concerned was made in 1953. Olivier and Richardson were due to leave the London organisation in 1949; it was agreed in the autumn of 1948 that Llewellyn Rees was to become administrator at the Old Vic. His first job would be to find a new director for the London company. It was natural, and in accordance with the 'ladder' system, which has been described in the previous chapter, and which Rees himself had done much to foster, that the choice should fall upon Hugh Hunt. The new appointment was announced before the end of 1948, and it was arranged that Hunt would leave Bristol in the spring of 1949.

He had gone a long way to fulfilling the promise that he made at that first public meeting where the formation of the Old Vic Company was announced. Whilst the reputation of the London company had, through an unfortunate train of circumstances, been declining, that of Bristol had been rising, and was steadily making its impact on the metropolitan *cognoscenti*. The London critics had been down to see the new plays performed by the company in the past few years; there had been two London showings. *Much Ado About Nothing* and *King Lear* had been seen at the Embassy Theatre in 1947; and *Hamlet* was brought to the St. James's Theatre as part of the Repertory Festival in 1948. None of these three productions, it must be admitted, had quite the same effect on the London audiences as that which they had exercised on the Bristol audiences; nevertheless they were judged on their own merits, and not patronisingly as the work of some poor country relation. The fact that there was this recognition of the company's status was the work of Hugh Hunt. By the time that he left he had, with his leadership, his keen sense of visualising the theatrical picture in a firm pattern, made his indelible stamp on the future of the Bristol Old Vic Company. A strong character, a good and true friend to all those who broke through the protective barrier of his outward reserve, he made enemies as well as comrades at Bristol; nevertheless in all the years of stress that were ahead of him he knew that he could always turn in solace to the West. His name has found its permanent place in the history of the Bristol Theatre, side by side with those of Palmer, Macready and Chute. Incidentally, during the four seasons of Hunt's period in command in Bristol, the theatre's income from all sources showed £1,300 profit over expenditure.

The management committee appointed Allan Davis as his successor. Davis had joined Hugh Hunt in the autumn of 1947 as production manager and assistant director. A young man under thirty, he carried with him an air of authority and determination. He had produced the Christmas plays and a few of the other plays; and his production of *Hedda Gabler* had won general praise, and particular acclaim from that peripatetic genius, Tyrone Guthrie, who happened to be on a visit to Bristol. Davis took over at Easter 1949, his final production of that season being Norman Ginsbury's *The School for Rivals*, which, since it was about Sheridan, was specially written with an eye to the Bath Festival, where it was played after the end of the Bristol season.

Guthrie, incidentally, had been invited to Bristol to discuss with the University authorities the progress of the Department of Drama, which was then in its infancy. The only such department within the faculties of arts in any British university, it stressed from the outset that its aims were not those of the dramatic academies and theatre schools. 'The professional schools are mainly concerned with presenting the art; the University mainly with the significance of what is being presented.'

One of Hunt's achievements, before he left Bristol, was to ensure that the University Drama Department worked in close contact with the Bristol Old Vic Theatre School, and this contact has since been developed by the able present head of the Drama Department, Dr. Glynne Wickham (who, incidentally, is a direct descendant of W. E. Gladstone). He had said more than once that the progress of the department, which has been spectacular, would not, despite its Rockefeller grant, have been possible without the collaboration of the Bristol Old Vic Company and its School.

The School during the year 1948-9 entered its third season. Still confined in very cramped surroundings, it was, under Edward Stanley, making steady headway. J. B. Priestley had given his royalties from the company's production of *The Inspector Calls* to the School Scholarship Fund, and the Dartington Trust not only displayed a generous financial interest but also invited the students to produce plays at their Barn Theatre. The students of the first two years' course were nearly all successful in finding work in the repertory theatres scattered throughout the country.

In the autumn of 1948 a cloud 'no bigger than a man's hand' appeared upon the horizon. It started with a fire. The Hippodrome Theatre in Bristol was burnt out in a fierce conflagration, which lasted only about an hour. The authorities, intent on closing the stable door, examined the other theatres in Bristol, and came to the conclusion that the fire precautions of 1766 at the Theatre Royal were not quite up to date enough for 1948. There followed a six-page report, which, though very kindly in content, insomuch that it expressed its desire to preserve historic amenities, was nevertheless firm on the question of security. Extensive alterations would have to be made, including the provision of fire-resisting doors, drencher systems, extra exits and a secondary lighting system. The architect's first rough calculation of the cost was the approximate figure of £20,000. Thanks to the confidence placed in Tom Hickson by the authorities, the theatre was given until the following summer before completing the repairs.

Sir Philip Morris took the matter firmly in hand. He grouped the requisitions into the 'practical' and the 'impractical', and as a result the police made considerable concessions in their requirements. This accomplished, I was instructed, as general manager, to put the position before the Arts Council.

It was a heavy responsibility which the Arts Council were being asked to undertake. They had, over the previous years, laboriously built up a reserve fund for building purposes. The work at Bristol would consume the whole of these savings. However, after some show of reluctance, it was agreed late in 1948 that the Council should shoulder this responsibility, and that the work was to commence in the summer break of 1949. [C.L.]

Sheridan's *The Rivals*, set in adjacent Bath, opened the Bristol Old Vic season on September 6th, and broke the Wilde tradition with a classic of youthful virtuosity (it was Sheridan's first comedy, written at the age of twenty-three). John Byron (Faulkland), Nigel Stock (Captain Absolute), David Phethean (Acres), John Phillips (Lucius), Janet Burnell (Mrs. Malaprop), Jill Balcon (Lydia) and Vera Lindsay (Julia) were new members of the company, with Paul Rogers as Sir Anthony Absolute (a 'sun-dappled volcano'—'a Wagnerian symphony of port and mustard-plaster') and Jane Wenham as Lucy to remind the audience of last season's favourites.

There is small doubt that John Byron's Faulkland dominated in quality. Alan Dent thought it (and Paul Rogers supports him) the finest of the performances; the others affected him horticulturally. David Phethean's Bob Acres, he wrote, was 'as earthy as a turnip', Jill Balcon's Lydia 'as dim as a violet', Vera Lindsay's Julia 'as arch as an iris, and as handsome'. In fact Vera Lindsay, a dark, Russian-born actress who had played for the London Mask Theatre under the name of Vera Poliakoff before the war, was too tragic in type and style for the elegances of eighteenth-century comedy, though Jane Wenham, piquant and tiny, as Lucy was perfectly cast. Janet Burnell, who had done fine work as leading actress at the Palmer's Green Intimate Theatre, also found Mrs. Malaprop within her range: she 'sweeps through it like a rose-and-feather-crowned tornado', wrote John Bennett.

The play was a suitable one for the Theatre Royal, with which it was almost contemporary, but this Hunt production designed by Alan Barlow was not as a whole more than average. Byron, who had been a ballet dancer, arranged the dances with professional skill.

A Month in the Country, by Turgenev, had in an adaptation by Emlyn Williams achieved success at the St. James's Theatre in 1943, with Valerie Taylor as Natalia and Michael Redgrave as Rakitin. Hunt now tackled its languorous Russian country-house atmosphere, but the comedy which many have found lurking satirically in Natalia—that lovely lily-of-the-field who brings love's heartache to infatuation and enraging caprice to friendship—could hardly emerge from the casting of Vera Lindsay in the part. She was, according to Coe, 'moving in anguish', but the *Western Daily Press* thought her ill-equipped vocally to convey the charm of Natalia: 'her moody unrest was mere petulance'.

John Byron's Rakitin was more at home in the semi-Tchehovian, semi-Gogol atmosphere ('One of the most unselfish pieces of acting I remember, exquisitely timed', wrote John Garrett), and Jane Wenham's Vera was an enchanting and touching picture of young girlhood shattered in the very act of emerging into a glowing womanhood. Paul Rogers's cynical doctor was also outstanding: 'John Phillips came nearer to what Natalia's husband should be than his disappointing Sir Lucius O'Trigger', wrote Garrett, 'but he failed to create imaginatively all that background of efficient and active life on the estate, outside and beyond the play, that was the strength of Paul Rogers's doctor. When the doctor confessed the man he is as he proposed marriage, no item in the catalogue of his shortcomings comes as a surprise—it is implicit in every stage of his previous performance. His acting in the scenes with the landowner (shades of Aguecheek) and with his future wife (faultlessly played by Janet Burnell) was triumphant —perhaps the more so because he was inducing lesser players than himself to play almost better than they knew how.'

Nigel Stock, as later with the London Old Vic (where Rogers and Jane Wenham changed their roles to Schaaf, the German tutor, and the little maid Katya), played the shy young tutor Beliaev, who causes so much upheaval, and Brian Smith, who before and after also shone with the London Old Vic Company as a child actor, played Kolia, Natalia's small son. The production owed much to Vera Lindsay, who was born in St. Petersburg and was able to give Hunt authentic advice (this versatile actress had also acted as a War Correspondent in the Normandy invasion and had followed the invading armies through in this capacity to the Nuremberg trials). It was 'tender, moving and richly humorous', wrote the *Western Daily Press*, which described the play as 'enchanting'. 'Anyone who is bored with it is bored by life itself.'

A Midsummer Night's Dream on October 9th was produced by Hugh Hunt with designs by Alan Barlow, and the Englishness of the fairies and background was stressed. The Puck of Stuart Burge was an attractive little pot-bellied monster, a horned Pan; the fairies often dark elves; the setting of blues and greens dominated by a hollow tree. 'Mr. Barlow's imaginative décor created just that fairyland, even down to the dew-pearl'd spiders' webs. After watching Oberon melt into the background of hollow tree and withered branch, one could forgive the first night recalcitrancy of the quarter moon which was clearly bewitched by Titania's beauty.' John Coe's praise was supplemented by Dennis Bushell: 'Mr. Hunt has made this play what it should be—a thing of beauty wrapped in warm, English humour.' Only Garrett demurred, complaining that the play was a dream, not a Freudian nightmare.

The music of John Dalby (a nineteen-year-old Bristolian and member of the Bristol Old Vic School) set the English note with its madrigalian quality: composed for five instruments, it was played backstage and relayed to the audience through a loudspeaker. John Byron arranged the dances, with patterns of fairy wand-lights in the last scene and a vigorous Burgomasque. He also played Oberon: 'beautifully spoken and moving', according to one of his colleagues, and darkly glittering beside Jill Balcon's classically brunette Titania. 'Miss Balcon and Mr. Byron did full justice to the glory of the poetry which falls to them, and gave to the production the shape and dignified form which it undoubtedly had', wrote Garrett.

Paul Rogers's young Devonshire Bottom, which he was to repeat at the London Old Vic later, and Nigel Stock's Quince also received high praise. 'Mr. Rogers has endeared himself so much to the playgoer that he has only to move a muscle of his handsome face to produce a gurgle of laughter', wrote John Coe, but Garrett thought the best performance was Stock's Quince, 'pathetic, endearing, a little lacking in wits, and challenged by occasion and opportunity, for which, in the dark watches of the night, he doubts whether he has the necessary equipment'. Jane Wenham's small dark Hermia (which was also seen later at the London Vic) was 'full of spirit', and Vera Lindsay as Helena displayed 'an unexpected sense of comedy'.

Maxwell Anderson's *Winterset*, which followed on November 9th, was a notable modern American tragedy which had been made into a fine film by the New York Group Theatre, but has still never been seen on the London stage. It was a triumph not only in itself but for Nigel Stock, of whose performance as the young hero Mio this word 'triumph' was actually used by all three Bristol critics and in several headlines. 'This is Young America in person, standing firm-footed', wrote the *Western Daily Press*. 'He pulses with sincerity. I shall long remember that blinding moment when he finds the truth and his voice rings out: "Now I know!" ' added Bennett. 'A great piece of acting, as good as anything I remember in the last six years', clinched Garrett.

The play is a verse-tragedy founded on an actual American case of misplaced justice (the Sacco and Vanzetti trial), and concerns the search of an Italian-American youth for the murderers who allowed his innocent father to be executed for their crime. It is a gangster story with a very great difference and an exciting plot, moving on two planes of violent action and human mystery and justice. Not only John Garrett recalled *Hamlet*, and referred to its poetic power of language. The setting—not unlike Arthur Miller's later play *A View from the Bridge*—is the squalid Italian quarter of New York's waterfront, and one scene (it was an artistically famous one in the American production) takes place on Brooklyn Bridge.

Owing to Hunt's absence in London producing *The Cherry Orchard* for the Old Vic Company at the New Theatre, *Winterset* was directed by Allan Davis with remarkable effect, helped by the brilliantly atmospheric settings of Larry Eggleton. 'In this memorable production by Allan Davis', wrote the *Western Daily Press*, 'there is as much unity of space as of action, the eye becoming a camera which views this waterfront scene from different angles.' And John Garrett emphasised the producer's skill: 'Mr. Davis's grouping, detail, timing, calculation of surprise, and control of the three climaxes in the second act were impeccable.'

Apart from Nigel Stock, the play was also a triumph for John Phillips, who repeated in Bristol the striking performance of the mad Judge Gaunt which he had created in the Birmingham Repertory production. Paul Rogers played the elderly Rabbi Esdras, a tragic figure who had been acted by his old dramatic teacher, Michael Chekhov, in the film. The gangster Trock was John Byron (not altogether suited), Jill Balcon the Rabbi's daughter Miriamne, and David Phethean his guilt-ridden and frightened son. Jane Wenham, who played Miriamne in another production of this play, had the small part of an old Italian apple-vendor.

Somerset Maugham's classic comedy *The Circle* could not have demanded a greater contrast of style. Produced by Edward Stanley on November 29th, it was notable for a splendid performance by Nuna Davey as Lady Kitty and excellent ones by Paul Rogers ('looking like a more than usually lugubrious Dalmatian') as Lord Porteous and by John Phillips as Clive Champion-Cheyney.

John Byron, too, excelled in the elegant priggishness of the husband, Arnold Champion-Cheyney, which John Gielgud had played with such wit in town. 'The Bristol Company', wrote Alan Dent, 'is settling down to be a capital team'.

Cinderella more than repeated the previous year's Christmas success, *Aladdin*. With music by Walter Leigh and Gavin Gordon (composer of the British ballet *The Rake's Progress*), it romped home with Rogers and Byron as Ugly Sisters and a *ballet blanc* so wondrously 'serious' that its satire of the real thing reached only the knowledgeable few, and many of the local audience were genuinely enraptured. Beatrice Appleyard, who directed the dances (with a *corps de ballet* of startling discrepancy of height and arrangement), also shone as the Attendant Imp of the Demon Gumboil (John Phillips), and Nuna Davey, in Mary Pickford curls, was a Queen Snowflake even more 'beautiful' than her Fairy Dew-Drop of the previous year (the fact that she wore a wedding ring perhaps added to her sentimental charm). Jill Balcon was a handsome Dandini, Nigel Stock a great success as a youthful Buttons who won and thrived on the audience's sympathy, and Jane Wenham an 'entrancing' Cinderella: sweet of voice and able to suggest both the wistfulness and helplessness of the character. As for Rogers (in blonde pigtails or Marie Antoinette ball finery: 'rugged, raddled and rampageous') and Byron ('fluttering, frilly and frolicsome'), their success was immediate, resounding and unforgotten.

John Byron's transformation to his next part, Romeo, was perhaps even more startling than Paul Rogers's to Tybalt (described by Dennis Bushell as 'a streak of envenomed black'). But the emphasis in this case was on the producer, for it was Hunt's last production for the Bristol Old Vic (he had been appointed Director of the London Old Vic from the coming autumn).

'Verona, as Hugh Hunt imagines it and Alan Barlow has painted it', wrote J. C. Trewin, 'glows with heat and colour: this is Italy indeed, fit for the romantic passion, verse that hangs upon the cheek of night and for the brawling passions of noon . . . the very heart of Verona.

'The play must also have, as Shaw has said, an " irresistibly impetuous march of music". There are few fine voices at the Theatre Royal but the company does not fumble, and John Byron

(Romeo) and Jane Wenham (Juliet), even if they miss something of the lyric ardour, rightly let the verse bear them forward.'

The Times found the finale 'pictorially most impressive, with the citizens of Verona peering through the grille of Capulet's vault and reflecting, no doubt with some complacency, for they have suffered much, on the grim scene within'. But the critic felt the production as a whole 'the picture of the world one sees within the camera obscura—precise, ranging, detailed, even in colour, but never the real, palpable living thing'.

Undoubtedly the production and performance were not a complete success, nor was the casting ideal. 'Mr. John Byron's Romeo leans to poetry but at the expense of Romeo, whose pangs like swords sink all too readily into a uniform melancholy', analysed *The Times*, and it was certainly a source of the tragedy's lack of passion and drive. But Jane Wenham's fresh and touching young Juliet carried a more authentic note: 'Miss Jane Wenham's Juliet is not to be passed over. She gets quite half of the character, which means that she may hope to add another quarter to it, for three-quarters of the part seems the most any one actress can give us. Even the potion scene she nearly brings off by playing much of it down, as if its terrors were almost too great for her to put into words.' (It was, it is curious to note now, Galina Ulanova's way: an interpretation in the Russian ballet 'out of this world' and brought to a synthesis of lyric transportation, beyond mere earthly terror, by a great artist at the height and flower of her genius.) 'Her study', wrote a Bristol critic of Jane Wenham, 'has eloquence in its silences and its speech, and a calm serenity that pervades the whole'; and another was wholly charmed: 'This young actress has a wistful, affecting quality, which accentuates Juliet's child-like vulnerability. It was a lovely performance.'

The most successful performance after the Juliet was perhaps Nuna Davey's Nurse: 'a comfortable cushion of an Italian woman', wrote Trewin, with some elements of the younger, more sex-conscious interpretation used by Wynne Clark in Robert Helpmann's later production for the London Old Vic. Rolf Lefebvre's Capulet was also widely praised, and Nigel Stock, the Mercutio, arranged some exciting and dangerous duels (both he and Rogers as Tybalt were frequent casualties in the cause of realism), although his Queen Mab speech suffered from a rather strained delivery.

Hamlet, 1948. Jane Wenham as Ophelia.

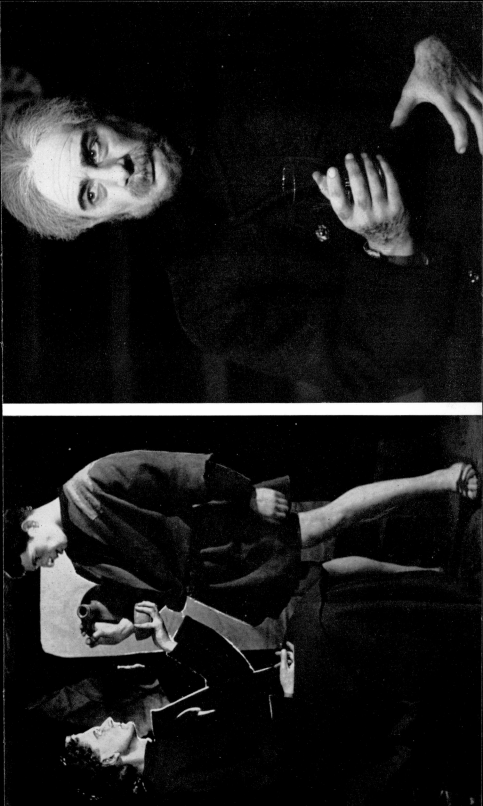

The Apple Orchards (Leonid Leonof), 1948. L. *to* R. round the table, Donald Sinden, Jane Wenham, Christopher Page, Leslie Sands, Richard Longman, Robert Eddison (centre back), Nuna Davey, Allan Cuthbertson, John Glen, Elizabeth Sellars, Rolf Lefebvre, Catherine Lacey.

OVER: (left) *Tobias and the Angel* (James Bridie), 1948. Robert Eddison as the Archangel Raphael and Paul Rogers (right) as Tobias. (right) *The Apple Orchards* (Leonid Leonof), 1948. Paul Rogers as Matvey Pwilyayef.

All photos by Desmond Tripp

Romeo and Juliet ran for four weeks from February 15th, 1949. It was succeeded on March 22nd by *Wilderness of Monkeys*, which Peter Watling had written for Paul Rogers and the Bristol Old Vic Company following the production of his *Rain on the Just* there the previous season. *Rain on the Just* was the better play, although *The Times*, when the Bristol production moved to the Embassy Theatre for a Repertory Festival in July, felt *Wilderness of Monkeys* fulfilled the hopes aroused by the earlier play. Rogers played the conscientious housemaster, Denys Reynolds, with the fine-drawn discipline and gentleness of one dedicated to classic literature and the classic way of life ('both the scholar's gentleness and his enthusiasm are deftly presented', wrote Harold Hobson), and Nigel Stock made a success of a sensitive schoolboy. 'Every posture, gesture and tone was perfectly attuned to his shapeless flannel suit, his bulging pockets and his unruly hair', wrote the *Western Daily Press*; and Philip Hope-Wallace in the *Manchester Guardian* during the Embassy season gave a special accolade to the two actors. 'These parts are played by Nigel Stock and Paul Rogers with a skill surpassing anything seen hitherto at this festival.' Nuna Davey as Lady Hildebrand 'sailed the sea superbly', in Hobson's phrase, and Sonia Williams, succeeding Jill Balcon, made her first appearance with the company as Phyllis Haslam (later she was to marry her fellow player, Nigel Stock). Allan Davis, now officially nominated Hugh Hunt's successor, produced the play, and also *The Jealous Wife* and *Arms and the Man* which followed.

The Jealous Wife, based by George Colman on Fielding's novel *Tom Jones*, is one of the lesser-known eighteenth-century comedies in the modern repertoire; Davis described it as 'an Easter pantomime, by the Clinton-Baddeley of the eighteenth century', and produced it with many contemporary stage devices including shutters and sliding wings, with the 'stage divided into sections, each representing the location of a scene, and as a scene finishes the shutters, on which the background is painted, will slide back to reveal the next scene, already set'.

The result, according to the *Western Daily Press*, was an action 'tempest-tossed, rowdy and boisterous like a Hogarth painting come to life, with Paul Rogers suitably Hogarthian in a robustious performance in perfect tune with the angle of Sir Harry Beagle's nose'. Nigel Stock achieved a triumphant 'double' as Mr. Oakley

73

and Captain O'Cutter: 'he has scarcely left the stage with the meek, twinkling steps proper to a man dancing deferential attendance on a whirlwind of a wife, before he has reappeared in the guise of a sea captain brandishing an Irish brogue above the whisperings and nudgings taking place among the bemused audience'. John Phillips played Major Oakley, John Byron the fop Lord Trinket, Nuna Davey Lady Freelove and Jane Wenham Harriet. Alan Barlow again designed the sets.

Arms and the Man, on May 2nd, 1949, was by general consent, like Olivia's complexion, 'exceedingly well done', the admirably balanced cast consisting of Paul Rogers (ideally cast as Captain Bluntschli), Sonia Williams (Raina), John Byron (Sergius), Jane Wenham (Louka), Nuna Davey (Catherine Petkoff), John Phillips (Major Petkoff) and Nigel Stock (Nicola). Byron, in eloquent moustache, was outstanding and compared favourably with Laurence Olivier in the same part for the major Vic company, and Rogers's Bluntschli, likewise, according to John Coe, 'had every right to be measured against the notable performance in London (by Ralph Richardson) during the war'. 'Some of the company's bombast overreached itself into bellow', wrote the *Western Daily Press* more cautiously, 'but nothing could have been more lilting and soothing than the varied music of the duet between Mr. Rogers and Miss Williams, the one so blunt and plausible, the other with such charm and sense of humour . . . these two played with exquisite understanding'. Rogers, indeed, thought his Raina as 'splendid' as Byron's Sergius, and responded to the inspired 'give-and-take' that such an acting partnership always encourages. The background of mountain peaks in Joyce Hammond's set gave an attractive effect of distance to the stage view and added colour and charm to the production.

The last play of the season, *The School for Rivals*, by Norman Ginsbury, was commissioned for the Bath Festival and opened in that city on May 23rd, 1949, and at Bristol a week later. A *pièce d'occasion* on the elopement of Elizabeth Linley with the dramatist Sheridan from Bath, it was not in the same dramatic class as Ginsbury's *Viceroy Sarah* and *The First Gentleman*, and both company and press were unfestively depressed. 'Mr. Ginsbury is not concerned with the delineation of incipient genius', complained *The Times*: 'He has merely written a romantic chronicle, not a comedy, not even a very entertaining play. For the air of

Bath is so notoriously relaxing that even playwrights may breathe of it and nod.'

Stock played the too-nebulous Sheridan, with Yvonne Mitchell as the black-eyed Elizabeth and Paul Rogers as the scientist Dr. Priestley—something nearer a full character part although he had no bearing whatever on the actual story. John Burrell produced without inspiration.

On Sunday, June 5th, a farewell meeting was given by the Old Vic Theatre Club to Hugh Hunt at the Theatre Royal, and a presentation made to the producer who had done so much to build the Bristol Old Vic, from its very foundations, into a strong artistic entity. He left to direct the London Old Vic at the New Theatre, taking his audience's grateful good wishes and also Nigel Stock, Paul Rogers and Jane Wenham with him. The fertilisation process between Bristol and London had already begun, and was to extend in later years to the artistic gain of both theatres.

In the meantime, the Bristol Royal was closed from the last performance of the season, on June 11th, 1949, until January the following year, for constructional alterations to meet the local council's fire regulations. When it reopened on January 5th, only Sonia Williams remained from among the leading players of the fourth season's company.   [A.W.]

CHAPTER SIX

The Fifth Season
1950

THE FIFTH SEASON did not open until January 1950. The theatre
had been closed for seven months, and in August 1949, when it
had been the centre of a fierce controversy which had swept
through the pages of *The Times* and other national papers, it
had seemed unlikely that it would open its doors again as a living
theatre. The future status indicated for it was that of a sedate
museum-piece.

As already indicated, the Arts Council had agreed to accept
the responsibility for the vast cost of repairs involved in the police
requisitions. Mr. Edwards, the architect, maintained that with
such an ancient building it was quite impossible to give a definite
estimate, although he stuck to his approximate figure of £20,000,
and, in the end, he was proved to be right. He came to London,
addressed the Council by means of plans pinned to a blackboard,
and his personality gave them reassurance. The go-ahead was given
for work to begin in June 1949. It started to date, but three weeks
later it was stopped.

Up till that date all repair work in the theatre, which since
1942 had totalled some £14,000 had been met by profits from the
running of the theatre, and the Council's funds had not been
called upon. At that very moment when, with great reluctance,
they had undertaken this new responsibility, the bill for which they
knew could not be met by theatre funds, the Council were presented with another account for £4,000, for work which, quite
apart from the requisitions, had been carried out in the theatre
during the previous year. There is no point in glossing over the
fact that they had not been informed that this work had been
undertaken.

The truth was that ever since the time of my appointment by
Lord Keynes in 1942, I had had a free hand in the maintenance
of the building. I acted on behalf of the Arts Council, and the
management committee, until the time of this incident, were not

76

involved in building affairs. So far, I had always paid for the expenditure out of the running profits; but this particular bill, for a new internal staircase, was, for various unavoidable reasons, double the expected costs, and when the account was presented there were insufficient funds in the Theatre Royal kitty to meet it.

The Arts Council panicked and decided to suspend all work on the requisitions. They said that they must obtain a firm estimate, though the experts assured them that this was impossible. Then they insisted that the Bristol Corporation should foot the bill, but the Local Government Act enabling money to be spent out of the rates on entertainment was only a year old, and the Bristol Corporation, in common with 98 per cent. of the other corporations in the country, were not yet attuned to the idea of this new form of expenditure.

The matter might have been smoothed out in reasonable discussion, and certainly there was no more patient and resourceful man than the chairman at the Bristol end, Sir Philip Morris; but theatre politics, whose intricacies it would be futile to trace at this moment, were at work. Among a section of the Arts Council there was a deep-rooted antipathy to the Old Vic and all its connections. It was this section that for a time prevented any settlement of the vexed question, but sought to put an end to the Bristol Old Vic Company by converting the theatre into a museum. This section forced the pace, and early in August it was decided to dismiss the skeleton staff at the theatre, whose constitution Sir Philip Morris's committee had worked out with care and economical forethought.

It quickly leaked out that Mr. Hickson and his staff were under notice, and then the Press storm burst in Bristol. The local papers made it clear that the citizens of Bristol had no intention of losing either the theatre or the company. They asked quite rightly why the Arts Council, if it feared the expense, had not made this clear when the matter was first broached to them in the previous autumn, instead of leaving their decision to this late date. *The Times* took the matter up in a leading article, and for three weeks the story was front-page news in the whole national Press. Through all the turmoil, the Council sat in bewildered but dignified silence. The 'Anti-Vic' section were in fact nonplussed. Seated in their metropolitan fastnesses, they had not realised the extent of the hold that the company had gained on the affections of the West.

It was the common sense of Sir Philip Morris which eventually found the way to a compromise. He came up to a meeting in London and suggested that the Council should send its deputy secretary, Mr. McRobert, to Bristol to investigate. Mr. McRobert hit on the happy expedient of splitting the estimates into two portions; one half was to be in ascertainable figures, the other half approximate. The total still came to the round figure of £20,000, but the Council grasped this face-saver and the work was put in hand. The total bill eventually came to £18,000.

One happy result of this controversy was an approach to the Bristol Corporation. Robert Lyne, who was then Chairman of the Bristol Old Vic Club, and was to be Lord Mayor of Bristol in the following year, paved the way to a meeting, and it was eventually agreed that the Corporation should contribute to future expenditure, both of the building and the company, and, in return, it was to have two representatives on the management committee. Since that date, Alderman F. G. W. Chamberlain (popularly known as 'Roy') has been one of the members of the management committee, and he has been a tower of strength as chairman of both the school and theatre building sub-committee.

The theatre reopened in January 1950 with Allan Davis's production of *As You Like It*. The audience were amazed, after all the controversy, to see so little change in the theatre. The auditorium had, in fact, been unaffected by the requisitions, and most of the alterations were behind stage, or in the side exits. It was a hectic night, with a group of civic visitors, who were the guests of the Corporation, unable to find their right seats, whilst the stage manager, anxious to ring up the curtain, fretted and fumed. Eventually the curtain rose on a new season and a new director.   [C.L.]

The directorship of Allan Davis formed only a brief interlude between the major periods of direction under Hugh Hunt and Denis Carey.

Davis's opening production of *As You Like It* on January 5th, 1950, attracted wide critical attention, and although it was not an outstanding success in itself ('It did not quite generate the warmth that comes from a sunlit mind', wrote John Coe, and Patrick Gibbs of the *Telegraph* thought the Arden 'a very petrified forest') it served to introduce to the Bristol Old Vic several players of considerable future interest.

Most notable, perhaps, was the nineteen-year-old diminutive Phebe, Dorothy Tutin, straight from R.A.D.A. and already magnetising response from the critics. Gibbs thought her 'passionately sincere', John Bennett 'sombre and brooding', the *Western Daily Press* 'a coquettish gipsy'. Frances Rowe, the Rosalind, was an actress of warmth and poise to whom success had come rather late and in America, where she had been chosen by Maurice Evans to play Ann Whitefield in his production of *Man and Superman.* Earlier, she had been notable for a performance of fascinating and serene maturity as the three-hundred-year-old Mrs. Lutestring and Lilith of Shaw's *Back to Methuselah* at the Arts Theatre. Her Rosalind was, according to Gibbs, 'fluent if not quite light enough', and indeed one would say her natural personality and distinctive qualities are not those of Rosalind. Yet *The Times* found it best 'when it was most vivacious, and her involuntary attestation of love in the mock courtship with Orlando came off delightfully. But her laughter and her tenderness at other times seemed to lack the proper lyrical quality'.

Nevertheless, here was a new leading lady of obvious distinction. Another newcomer, Dennis Cannan, who played 'a pretty villian' as Oliver, was to gain Bristol and London distinction in another capacity than acting; as 'Denis Cannan' (repudiating an 'n') he was to be the author of *Captain Carvallo*, which had its first production at the Bristol Old Vic this season, and later achieved West End success.

The major character actor was George Coulouris, back from Hollywood to play Jaques and later Molière's Tartuffe; the romantic lead David King-Wood, who had played leading parts at Stratford-on-Avon a few years before (*The Times* thought him 'a finely romantic Orlando, meeting tyranny with spirit and speaking the love verse excellently'). Another character actor, Wensley Pithey, acted 'an exuberant, extraverted Touchstone, played with an effective mixture of subtlety and gusto'. Emrys Jones, a young actor well known already in London, was content here with the small part of Charles the Wrestler. The Duke Frederick, Kenneth Mackintosh, has been a leading player since at the Birmingham Repertory Theatre, achieving special distinction for his ironic prologue as the God Ra in the production of *Caesar and Cleopatra* brought by the Birmingham company to the Old Vic in the summer of 1956.

Two other actresses shone particularly: the ebullient and roguish Jessie Evans (also making her Bristol Old Vic début) as Audrey and Sonia Williams from last season, whose 'refreshing' Celia—'a little part which she picked out and made to live'— gave wide delight.

A new young designer, Hutchinson-Scott, was to stay long with the Bristol Old Vic. The customary Prologue at the opening of a new season was written on this occasion by Paul Dehn and spoken by Stephen Kaye in the character of Hymen.

Miles Malleson's 'free adaptations' of Molière, which have given new stage life to the French master's plays in this country, have regularly across the years been triumphantly successful at the Bristol Old Vic. *Tartuffe*, produced on February 21st, was the expected 'resounding triumph'. 'I have picked up the text', wrote Malleson, 'carried it across the English Channel and dropped in on England three hundred years later. Molière himself was an actor, and I am sure he would be the first to approve of what I have done to make his work live for another nation in another age.' The heavy intractability for both speaking and listening purposes of the average Molière English translation up to our time is Malleson's best justification; his colloquialisms may sometimes give the listener an out-of-period jar, but they are at least merry and comedic, easy on the actor's tongue, and make up in apt humour what they sometimes lack in astringency. The plays take the stage with wit and the characterisation blooms as it should, for Molière, like all great comic writers, draws people essentially outside time, and his wisdom and irony have more than a contemporary ring.

'George Coulouris's villain—though he is more Dickensian than Molièresque, more Chadband than Tartuffe—oozes satisfactorily, like a churn', wrote the *News Chronicle*; but *The Times* was more explicitly critical: 'Mr. George Coulouris plays Tartuffe as the eternal "confidence man". His reading of the part gives no encouragement to the theory that the greedy, lazy, licentious, self-seeking rogue is a man who besides deceiving others also deceives himself. Mr. Coulouris suggests the careful calculation of the thin-lipped lawyer. . . . There is nothing in this Tartuffe of Shakespeare's Angelo, nothing of the man who has strayed from the norm and allowed his natural instincts to become warped and perverted. Indeed, in the attempted seduction there is so little passion that we are tempted to think he is moved by nothing but casual greed, and the scene suffers thereby.'

Wensley Pithey played the ingenuous and jealous M. Orgon; Jessie Evans was a delicious Dorine; Frances Rowe a gracefully distinguished Elmire; and Dorothy Tutin, Emrys Jones, David King-Wood and Julian Randall played the younger people with spirit.

A prologue, adapted from Molière's *L'Impromptu de Versailles*, was performed before the play—the characters being the actors and actresses who perform in *Tartuffe* and the setting the stage of the Théâtre du Palais Royal, 1663. Davis produced, with settings and costumes by Hutchinson-Scott.

Cannan's *Captain Carvallo*, on March 14th, brought the company and theatre the genuine distinction of making a notable dramatist discovery. It was, in fact, Cannan's tenth play, eight of which he destroyed (the ninth, *Max*, had been performed at the Malvern Festival, where it attracted Allan Davis's attention). *Carvallo* had as its setting a mythical country, Arcadia, to which the dramatist was to return in a later play, *Misery Me!* It was a country in the throes of war, and its witty action in a mountain inn had more than an echo of Shaw's *Arms and the Man*. 'His play shimmers with ideas wittily juxtaposed, and it is funnier than the Crazy Gang', wrote Harold Hobson; its main defect was a tendency to lose the discussive thread in a bedroom farce which would have surprised Shaw and did not add to the cohesion of the play's rather wavering style. But its fireworks were sparkling enough to attract Laurence Olivier, who bought the play, and some crisp character parts stimulated the actors. Frances Rowe, in the part later played by Diana Wynyard, 'allies good looks and keen wits with a sharp sense of fun', approved Hobson; Emrys Jones played Carvallo and David King-Wood Professor Winke ('the acting triumph of the evening', according to the *Western Daily Press*). Coulouris was the Caspar Darde, John Moffatt the Private Gross, Wensley Pithey the Baron and Dorothy Tutin the pert maid Anni.

Barrie's *The Admirable Crichton*, a play that, more than most of his, holds its stage effect, followed on April 4th. It was the Bristol Old Vic's first Barrie play and the first production there of Allan Davis's assistant, Robert Quentin, who was later to work with Hugh Hunt at the London Old Vic.

'Does it bear revival?' queried the *Western Daily Press*. 'When

81

revived in such beautiful mounting and with such mellow devotion, there can be only one answer. The performance is elegantly Edwardian in spirit and the characters play the game without a smirk. Since every pause and every intonation is eloquent and there is no distraction to the eye or tedium to the mind, we can assume that Mr. Quentin has done his work unobtrusively and well. . . . Frances Rowe, whose intelligence, polish and resilience can now be taken for granted, adds to these qualities a warm radiance that makes her Lady Mary the most enchanting character she has yet drawn here, while Dorothy Tutin plays Tweeny with a waif-like, wide-eyed eagerness which is most affecting.'

High praise was also won by Coulouris as Crichton: 'He has tremendous presence, and limitless reserves of reposeful strength which are apt to account for the awe in which he was held by the castaways at the expense of their and the audience's affection.' Pithey played the Earl of Loam, King-Wood Lord Brocklehurst, and Daphne Heard a 'regal, diamond-glittering Countess of Brocklehurst'. The scenery was by Joyce Hammond.

Julius Caesar on April 25th was the brief season's Shakespearian choice, and with its demands for a large and powerful male cast in some measure defeated the company. Yet Davis's production, with crowd work by Edward Stanley and his Bristol Dramatic School students, had a certain flare and impact, with an emphasis on 'murder and mass-madness'. 'The sombre nature of the theme', wrote John Coe, 'is reflected in Mr. Hutchinson-Scott's settings, which are magnificent in scope and execution. The lurid sky, the massive pillars, and the cavernous tunnel all point to tragedy and awaken in the onlooker a sense of impending doom.'

The acting, according to Coe, focused on the Mark Antony of King-Wood, who in the words of the *Western Daily Press* also 'swept the play to its grand and awe-inspiring climax in a shower of dazzling poetry'. But this is the 'easy' part to play, as Irving (attracted more by Brutus) shrewdly realised; the difficulties lie with Cassius and Brutus, and Cassius, in particular, has been galvanised in our time by such actors as John Gielgud (vividly spotlighting the psychological twist and the rhetorical rhythm) and Paul Rogers. The Cassius here (Cecil Winter) was 'a snarling *provocateur*', a reading which always tends rather to diminish the character, for Cassius has a nobility not less tragic because it is flawed by envy, and both he and the Brutus of Coulouris were inclined to over-casual speaking. Dennis Cannan, released during the run to attend the *Captain Carvallo* rehearsals in London, doubled Caesar and Octavius with a certain success: 'Dennis Cannan's ashen-faced Caesar', wrote the *Western Daily Press*, 'is sufficiently full of egotistical rant and yet endued with a solemn dignity which of itself provides the extra chill of horror in a death scene which has him dangling like a fluttering rag from the base of the monument'.

Dorothy Tutin played Brutus's page Lucius, Daphne Heard Calpurnia and Frances Rowe Portia, and an interesting first appearance in the company was made by Paul Daneman (later to achieve outstanding success as a character actor at the Birmingham Repertory Theatre and as Justice Shallow at the London Old Vic), who trebled the parts of Cicero, Strato and the servant to Antony.

Sir John Vanbrugh's *The Provok'd Wife* had Bath associations: Mrs. Siddons made her first appearance there in the character of Lady Brute at a salary of £3 per week, all she could command after her first disastrous London failure. Quin, too, played Sir John Brute there, and forgot, it is said (unlike Cibber and Garrick) that a gentleman still lurked beneath the gusto and debauchery. The play certainly is strong in flavour ('almost coarse' was the unexpected euphemism of one Bristol critic), but the performance at the Bath Assembly (prior to Bristol) evoked a generous tribute from Richard Findlater in *The Tribune*:

How much wittier Vanbrugh's play seemed here, than in its recent revival at the Arts. And this was not only because of the general miscasting of the London production, but rather because of a difference of method. At the Arts the players strove for a period 'style', which is meaningless, a mere plaster-cast, without an understanding of the play and a respect for its dialogue. In Allan Davis's production at Bath several actors are 'out of period', but that doesn't seem to matter. They all give the text full emphasis, taking every warrant for sexual innuendo but doing so without a snigger, and they speak with relish and intelligence, though disposed to scurry. The result is a successful compromise which gives the play a fresh coat of paint, and brings out the contemporary vitality of the dialogue.

As the pert Belinda, who converts Heartfree to matrimony,

Dorothy Tutin delightfully combined the randy and the demure. In the early scenes Miss Tutin, handicapped by costume, seemed alarmingly under age, even for Vanbrugh's days, but she overcame the obstacle with an ease notable in so young an actress.

Findlater was also one of the first to notice the rising talent of Paul Daneman, who played Constant, 'a gentleman of the town'.

Coulouris's part of Brute was described elsewhere as being taken 'perhaps a little cautiously, but with that careful eye to detail we are accustomed to in this actor's work'. Frances Rowe played Lady Brute, Daphne Heard Lady Fanciful, and King-Wood Heartfree.

The play was produced for two weeks at Bristol on May 22nd, and the season ended in the week beginning June 5th with a revival of *Tartuffe*, in which Paul Daneman played Damis and John Phillips a Police Officer, but the cast otherwise remained unchanged. [A.W.]

CHAPTER SEVEN

The Sixth Season
1950 *to* 1951

ALLAN DAVIS was director at Bristol for only one season. In the summer of 1950, thanks to an introduction effected by Kenneth Rae, of the International Theatre Institute, he went to the United States on a University Drama Scholarship. After he had been in America for about a year he obtained a long-term contract at Hollywood as a trainee director; but the atmosphere of Filmland could not be very congenial to a theatre man—especially one who was 'Bristol bred'—and he returned to England late in 1953. Since then he has been a free-lance producer in the London and New York theatre, his most recent big success in London having been the direction of John Clements in the play *A Shadow of Doubt*.

In Bristol he will be remembered for his keenness in discovering new writers. He introduced Peter Watling, whose two plays, *Rain on the Just* and *A Wilderness of Monkeys* were produced during Hugh Hunt's régime. It was in every sense of the word a *coup de théâtre* on the part of Davis to include in his 1950 company at Bristol the young actor Dennis Cannan, whose first produced play *Max*, though confused in purpose, had caught the attention of the critics at the Malvern Festival. Cannan already had in his briefcase another play, *Captain Carvallo*, and this play (as already recorded) duly found its way into the spring 1950 programme. It was promptly bought by Laurence Olivier and produced by him at the St. James's Theatre in the autumn of 1950, and it is an open secret that the author preferred the production at Bristol. Dorothy Tutin, who had been cast as the maidservant at Bristol, was deemed to be too unknown for so important a role in London, and the part was not offered to her.

To succeed Davis, it was decided to appoint Denis Carey, a young man in the thirties, whose whole background had been in the 'cultural' theatre. An Irishman, his mother an actress at the Abbey Theatre, he had been destined for the Eire Civil Service; but luckily for the theatre, he had failed to pass his tests in Erse, although he had been sent to the furthermost tip of Europe, the Blasket Islands, to immerse himself in the language. Martin Browne, lecturing in Ireland, found Denis and brought him over to England to play in *Murder in the Cathedral* and during the war Denis was a stalwart of Martin Browne's Pilgrim Players, acting, stage managing, setting up and driving lorries in the arduous one-night-stand touring of that pioneer company. There followed work of a similar nature with various C.E.M.A. and Arts Council companies, and in 1943 he was a member of the opening company of Bridie's Glasgow Citizens' Theatre, and it was here that he met his wife, Yvonne Coulette. The end of the war found both of them members of the Midland Theatre Company, which opened at Coventry. He was beginning to be well known as a character actor, when Ashley Dukes gave him his first chance of production at the Mercury Theatre, and he distinguished himself with *Happy as Larry*, which was promptly transferred to the Criterion Theatre. A little later he joined Peter Potter as associate producer at the Arts Council Theatre at Salisbury, and here he was brought into intimate contact with all the personalities of the Arts Council and the Old Vic, who were at that time responsible to their respective organisations for the running of Bristol. No one could have failed to notice the atmosphere that pervaded at Salisbury. It is Denis's chief asset that he can always extract the best from his company by creating an aura of happiness. Only the briefest discussions were necessary before it was decided that Rees should nominate Carey to the management committee. It was a further example of the 'ladder' system at work.

It was resolved that Edward Stanley, who had by then had four years' experience with the organisation as director of the school should add to his duties as assistant director to Carey. Denis brought with him from Salisbury, as stage director, Nat Brenner, who is still with the company in 1957 as production manager. Carey had been to the theatre during the war years as an actor in a visiting company from the Glasgow Citizens', but otherwise had had no connection with Bristol. His discussions with Rees and his appointment had been made in London; and it was not until the day of the Press conference at which the appointment was to be announced that he came to the Theatre Royal. Shy and unassuming at first acquaintance, Denis knocked quietly at Mr. Hickson's door. Tom, fully occupied at the moment, saw a strange young man and said swiftly: 'I'm sorry, I can't see anyone just now. We have a Press conference to introduce the new director. If you like to wait, I'll attend to you in a little while.' So Denis, without saying a word, took a seat in the lounge, and sat there until he was rescued by Rees.

Used to the more experimental atmosphere at Salisbury, where plays were not judged so keenly for their box-office value, Denis started with a programme that reflected his own rather than public taste. He had played in Goldsmith's play *The Good-Natured Man* at Glasgow, and he placed it on his opening list at Bristol. He was warned that it was the literal truth that the failure of this play (the second production of the Citizens' Theatre in 1943) had come within an ace of closing that new venture down, but he persisted; and the box-office results at Bristol were equally disastrous. He was quick to learn his lesson, quick to learn the—to him—new responsibilities of administration, and he broadened in character, and his grasp became firmer. Under his direction, the Bristol Old Vic Company entered its most fruitful period.

A survey of this season would be incomplete without a reference to the school. In 1951 the *Bristol Evening Post*, which had always shown a great interest in the Bristol Old Vic Theatre School, established an annual award for the student nominated as the most promising in the First Year Course. The first such award was given to Phyllida Law, whose brilliant comedy work has since then fully justified her selection.   [C.L.]

Denis Carey's four seasons at the Bristol Old Vic were to be a period of further development and success, and they opened propitiously with the spring-like cadences of Christopher Fry's verse-play, *The Lady's Not For Burning*, on September 5th, 1950.

There were several important newcomers to the company, who were to make their mark on Old Vic history. John Neville, a tall, fair young actor from the Birmingham Repertory (where he admits to having had negligible success), was Richard, the part played by the young Richard Burton in town and full of May-morning music. Newton Blick, whose experience had ranged from variety to Shakespeare, was the richly characterised Mayor, Hebble Tyson. Pamela Alan, almost as widely experienced for a young actress (she had been one of Cochran's Young Ladies in *Big Ben*, had appeared in Shakespeare at Stratford-on-Avon and in

87

repertory at Guildford, and played under Denis Carey's guidance with the Pilgrim Players) was the heroine, Jennet Jourdemaine; Donald Pleasence, later to make his mark as a character actor, had the fairly small part of Humphrey Devize (with Donald Sinden back to play his brother Nicholas); Joan White was the mother, Margaret Devize; and Gudrun Ure (who later in her career changed her name to Ann Gudrun and played Desdemona to Orson Welles's Othello) was Richard's partner in spring music, the young Alizon Eliot. In addition, John Phillips returned to act Thomas Mendip (he was, according to the admiring young Neville, the 'ideal leading man'), and Stuart Burge to play the delightful chaplain ('as sweet and uncertain as church-bells on a windy day', in Fry's description).

'This play, as magical as the April sunlight that pours through the window of Mayor Tyson's house, was born out of its time', wrote Carey, the producer, in a programme note. 'It is the first completely lyrical play in the whole range of the English theatre. And it will last as long as our language does. By lyrical I do not mean that the dramatist does not make use of character and situation. Of course he does. But his first purpose is to *sing* . . . to weave his words and his characters into a pattern so that they sing and dance together. . . . And to increase this effect he has used every kind of light and shadow—sunlight, firelight, candlelight and moonlight—all in one fitful April day.'

Carey, wrote John Coe of the production, 'has gone for the comedy and made it ring'; John Bennett as decidedly declared he 'played the comedy in a minor key'! According to the *Western Daily Press*, yet again, the production had 'great power in its silences and stillness', at some sacrifice of vitality. All this probably meant was that Carey balanced the harmonies of the play itself, so that none predominated and all merged musically in tune. And the spring-tones rang sweetly in Hutchinson-Scott's setting, 'with its symbolic, rather than realistic lighting', described John Bennett, and its 'pastel shades, sometimes leaping into vivid contrast as when he let "the lady" step on the stage in a gown of flame velvet and gold'. Pamela Alan made an excellent first impression: a 'vivid, sultry study'—'her voice is of fine texture: her poise disciplined and confident'. And Bennett noticed 'from John Neville and Gudrun Ure we have two little gems of charm as the young lovers whose quiet romance is a tender side-plot'.

As You Like It, 1950. Dorothy Tutin as Phebe and Emrys
Jones as Silvius.

ABOVE: *Winterset* (Maxwell Anderson), 1948. Nigel Stock as Mio and Jill Balcon as Miriamne.

BELOW: *Captain Carvallo* (Denis Cannan), 1950. L. *to* R. Dorothy Tutin as Anni, Emrys Jones as Captain Carvallo and Frances Rowe as Smilja Darde.

Both photos by Desmond Tripp

Desmond Tripp

The Cocktail Party (T. S. Eliot), 1951. Gudrun Ure (now known as Ann Gudrun) as Celia Coplestone and Peter Coke as Edward Chamberlayne.

ABOVE: *The Provok'd Wife* (Vanbrugh), 1950. L. *to* R. David King-Wood as Heartfree, George Coulouris as Sir John Brute, Paul Daneman as Constant.

BELOW: *The Prodigious Snob* (Molière–Malleson), 1951. Miles Malleson (right) as M. Jourdain, Pamela Alan as Dorimène, Michael Aldridge as Dorante.

Both photos by Desmond Tripp

Goldsmith's *The Good-Natured Man*, which followed on September 26th, was an original choice of comedy, although the Old Vic Company had produced it on tour early in the war with Robert Donat as Mr. Croaker—a brilliant and highly praised comedy performance which did not save the play from the ill success at the box office which also attended its production at Glasgow and Bristol. It was first presented in 1768, two years after the opening of the Bristol Theatre Royal, and was, in Denis Carey's words, 'as robust a comedy as one could wish for'. Carey produced it in sepia backgrounds by Hutchinson-Scott, with a now-familiar programme phrase, 'Lighting by Nat Brenner', who was the new season's Stage Director. John Phillips's scarecrow Mr. Croaker was a great success, and Donald Pleasence also notably scored (in the words of the *Western Daily Press*) as Mr. Lofty, 'a Groucho Marx of the 1770s . . . a gaudy, undulating figure, absurdly pompous, who prowls glibly in the wake of his own fantasies'. Neville played Leontine, Croaker's son, with Blick, Pamela Alan, Joan White, Donald Sinden and Gudrun Ure in other parts.

Sixteenth-century England followed the eighteenth on October 17th, when Carey had his first Bristol shot at Shakespeare with *The Merry Wives of Windsor*. 'I cannot even read this play—and it was of course meant to be *acted*, written hurriedly in a fortnight, to order, for a rep. company something like ours, without a feeling of intoxication, of breath of another world, and of pure joy in being alive', wrote Carey in the programme. It is a reaction some people find difficult to share (Neville, languishing as Fenton, a romantic cipher of a part still remembered by the actor with bitterness, doubtless did not do so!); but it produced a rather slapstick production described as both 'rampageous' and 'hearty', and Newton Blick scored a success as Falstaff: 'a Father Christmas whose eyes are a rapacious declaration that it is more blessed to receive than to give'. Lally Bowers, an excellent comedy character actress new to the company (she was to shine in later years as Fairy Snowflake and in the Dorothy Reynolds parts in a second company playing *Salad Days*), was Mrs. Page, Pamela Alan Mrs. Ford, John Phillips a rather 'stern' and 'earnest' Ford, Donald Pleasence the Slender and Donald Sinden a Pistol with a 'harsh, resounding report'.

During the run, on October 30th, 1950, John Neville and his

89

wife, Caroline Hooper, presented the Bristol Old Vic with its first baby of the season; a daughter, the eldest of their delightful family, all loyally born or adopted under the Old Vic banner.

Blind Man's Buff, the first serious and also the first new play to be produced under the Carey régime, was a free adaptation of Ernst Toller's play, *The Blind Goddess*, by Denis Johnston, the Irish dramatist and author of *Weep for the Cyclops*. Three years later it reached the West End with two of the original Bristol players—John Phillips as the State Solicitor and Newton Blick as the Judge—in the cast. Both gave particularly fine performances: Phillips sensitively etching the reticent, cold man in authority who has the integrity to admit his own mistake, and Blick giving the Judge a telling and authoritative quietness.

It is a good play on a miscarriage of justice, weakened by the author's failure to win any sympathy, and therefore the audience's concern, for the doctor who is falsely accused of murder yet does everything to alienate his judges. The doctor sets a more than difficult task for the actor, and neither Donald Pleasence in Bristol nor Dennis Price in London could perhaps be blamed for failing to give it plausibility or emotional force. Pamela Alan as the woman doctor who thinks she loves him, until the truth of his character is revealed, had better chances, and (as Coe wrote), 'John Neville's study of a pathologist reluctant to admit a cardinal error was sharp and clear'. It was the actor's first serious acting part at Bristol: 'a real character' and a welcome relief from the type of romanticism which in spite of his splendidly appropriate looks he always finds rather irksome. For Phillips was reserved the highest praise: Beverley Baxter's comment in the *Sunday Express* that he 'moves and speaks like a king. Bristol is not big enough for this noble actor'.

Pinero's farce, *The Magistrate*, was Edward Stanley's first production since his appointment as Assistant Director to Carey. As in the case of *Blind Man's Buff*, Blick played the same part later at the St. Martin's Theatre in London. His Victorian Magistrate of impeccable reputation wrecked by farcical error was a brilliant comedy performance, and it shared critical praise with Donald Sinden's study of his more than adolescent stepson, forced by a mother intent on preserving her youth to pretend that he is only fourteen years old. Phillips, too, scored heavily as the retired Colonel Lukyn from Bengal—Neville describes his 'scientific' attitude to the playing of farce as a lesson and inspiration to his younger colleagues.

Perhaps it was this analytic attitude which enabled Phillips not only to act farce but to write it. For he was the author of the Christmas pantomime, *Puss in Boots*, which, tailored to the company and the Bristol Theatre Royal stage, opened on December 21st with music by Clifford Parker. Perhaps, too, it was not coincidental that he chose for himself the part of Catnip, described by a critic as bearing 'more than a superficial resemblance to Croaker'.

It was a pantomime of sixteen scenes and many wonders (the Eighth Wonder was the Royal Mail Train, the Ninth the Balloon and the Final the Telescope) and 'one feels instinctively', wrote the *Western Daily Press*, that the composer and author 'have a deeper affection for Gilbert and Sullivan than for Rodgers and Hammerstein II'. The Gilbertian (and pre-Gilbertian Planché) echo certainly rings in the two courtiers, High Factotum and Low Factotum, played by John Neville and Stuart Burge, and Neville, a red-haired tenor in a walrus moustache, also had considerable fun as Mr. Sandwickers, an inventor, accompanied by a wheezy Stephenson train. His Engine Driver's Song (sung in duet with Low Factotum) was one of the happier items of the show. Phillips as Catnip was 'marvellously funny', and Pamela Alan was the Principal Boy. 'Hugh Manning's ogre is a bad dream that must have emerged from the Kremlin', wrote Dennis Bushell, and the *Western Daily Press* toyed with another kind of Marxism: 'Donald Pleasence has already shown Marxist leanings, and here puts to brilliant effect what must surely be a lifelong study of Harpo.' Newton Blick sounds strangely fascinating as 'King Clovis of Brittany', Edward Burnham was Puss, Gudrun Ure the Princess Celia, and Pleasence and Donald Sinden brothers amiably christened Dusty and Rusty. Hutchinson-Scott's designs, according to Coe, had 'real enchantment'. Carey was the producer, and the dance-arrangers Muriel Carpenter (director of the active Bristol School of Dancing, widely known in the British ballet world) and Rafael Shelly.

Carey's predilection for comedy continued with *The School for Scandal* after Christmas, though Edward Stanley was again here the producer. John Phillips and Donald Sinden had left after the pantomime, and the new leading man, Peter Coke, played

91

Sir Peter Teazle. As Lady Teazle twenty-four-year-old Gudrun Ure was entrusted with her first leading Bristol Old Vic part. She was already an experienced actress who had appeared at Perth Repertory, the Glasgow Citizens' Theatre and the Edinburgh Festival. The *Western Daily Press* described her as 'somewhat less polished than is usual', but 'youthful and constantly reminding us of her country origin'. Coe thought the acting generally only 'serviceable', but praised Neville as 'an engaging Charles' (it was a new departure for the actor, who not only enjoyed the part but felt it one of the best things he did in Bristol). Pleasence was not ideally cast or plausible as Joseph Surface, though he caught something of the eighteenth-century manner, but Blick was the perfect Sir Oliver, lovable, expansive and irascible, and Denis Carey, making his only Bristol acting appearance as Crabtree, was described as savouring slightly of the Abbey, Dublin! Joan White was Mrs. Candour, Pamela Alan Lady Sneerwell and Scott the inevitable designer.

T. S. Eliot's *The Cocktail Party*, on March 13th, 1951, created a strong impression: though Bushell's headline in the *Evening World* was 'Enjoyable, But Unfathomable, Play at the Old Vic'! 'What you find in it depends on what you bring to it', Eliot has written; but certainly its 'Guardians' are altruistic figures, who unlike the Fates and Goddesses of Greek tragedy leave the human beings they guide and protect the element of personal choice. It is because Celia Coplestone's life of sacrifice was her choice, the right life for her, that her martyrdom, though moving, is bearable—for all its Greek elements of horror—in the theatre, and the part is a superb one for an actress of subdued passion. Gudrun Ure, more successful as Celia than as Lady Teazle, was described as giving 'the most moving performance by an Old Vic actress for years'—'a complete and compelling study'. To a colleague in the cast, Peter Coke's Edward Chamberlayne was nevertheless the outstanding performance ('The misfits', concurred the *Western Daily Press*, 'are generally better than the guardians, who rather lack power'). Pleasence played the Unidentified Guest, Joan White Mrs. Shuttlethwaite, Pamela Alan Lavinia Chamberlayne and John Neville Peter Quilpe.

'Denis Carey and the Bristol Old Vic solve their problems triumphantly. The solution is reached by having no inhibitions about a very slow tempo and a very low volume, tightening each to the highest strain of expectancy by almost every device known to the theatre', wrote the *Western Daily Press*. A new name appeared as designer: Pat Robertson, the assistant scenic artist, who was later to do much fine work for the Theatre Royal as its regular designer. His décor was described as 'the smartest of birdcages', and there was some criticism of the tight clothes which restricted the actresses' movements. Nevertheless, many were moved and enthusiastic: 'You really touched greatness', said Charles Landstone to the company at the end of the run.

Saint Joan, on April 3rd, brought another play of serious weight and content, produced by Carey in 'a succession of beautifully lighted and artistic settings'. ('To convey a cathedral with one pillar and ornamental ironwork is an example of his craft', wrote John Bennett of Hutchinson-Scott.) Inevitably, however, the impression depended on the Joan, Pamela Alan, whom Bennett found moving, sincere, quiet, persuasive, but not giving 'a strong enough reading to take its place in the trial scene'. The *Western Daily Press*, on the other hand, thought it 'a lovely performance . . . in her boyishness there is the true crusading zeal. Yet she does not neglect the spiritual side. Leaning against a pillar in Rheims Cathedral, she is rapt indeed'.

The most unequivocal success was Donald Pleasence's Dauphin, which Coe thought brilliant, and which prepared the way for the same actor's Dauphin in the London production of Anouilh's *The Lark* five years later. The Irish actor Michael Golden joined the company to play Cauchon, and Wolfe Morris, the De Stogumber, was also new to Bristol. John Neville was the Dunois and Peter Coke Warwick, while Hugh Manning won praise for his 'thoughtful and exquisitely phrased address' as the Inquisitor.

Denis Carey, writing of *The Kreutzer Sonata* some weeks before its production, had described it as 'the most exciting new play we have read this season'. Unfortunately, criticisms did not bear out this optimistic estimate, and a member of the cast years later described it, with some feeling, as an 'earth-shaking failure' and his most embarrassing stage experience. Certainly all did not run smoothly behind-scenes. The play was an adaptation by two authors, Eugen Ilyin and Charlotte Frances, of Tolstoy's rather unpleasant sex-story of the same title (taken, of course, from Beethoven, a chief character being a philandering violinist— Tolstoy at the time being in one of his more puritanical moods regarding the moral decadence of the arts and the emotions to which they give rise). But as Tolstoy's novel was of only extended-short-story length, a completely apocryphal third act had been added by the dramatists in the nature of a murder trial. It was on this act that the play apparently mainly foundered, but the fall was fatal. The first half of the play was described by the *Western Daily Press* as of 'considerable interest and dramatic intensity. Then melodrama reared its ugly head: and the last act was a muddle so dismal that one was astonished no better subject could be found for the Bristol Old Vic's admirable policy of bringing fresh work to the theatre'. Coe also thought the court-room scene 'a crashing anticlimax'.

Tony Britton joined the company to play the reticent, self-sacrificing Doctor Ivan Zakharwitch; he was a twenty-six-year-old actor from the local town of Weston-super-Mare, who had acted under Peter Cotes at the Manchester Library Theatre and had walked into Carey's office purely 'on spec'. Peter Coke and Pamela Alan as the husband and wife were both well praised, and John Bennett thought Neville's violinist 'young and ardent'.

The season ended less lugubriously with Carey's production of *The Taming of the Shrew*, a 'romp' he was to repeat some years later at the London Old Vic. The Bristol variations included, we read, 'missing scene-shifters, strings of actors moving speedily in and out and round about like the people in the Cornish Floral Dance, sprightly lackeys doing Tarzan acts on tables and chairs; and other pretty conceits'. It was a mixture of the Marx Brothers and Crazy Gang, set in a single Hutchinson-Scott setting showing 'the roof-line of Padua sweeping round backstage, so that the characters come on silhouetted against the azure sky'. 'The production', wrote Bushell 'goes off like a rocket and maintains a brilliant flight to the finish.'

It is true John Garrett rumbled ominously about the omission of the Induction—'wickedness', 'tinkering', 'mutilation' (heavy words for so light a farce?). But Peter Coke's 'exuberant, vital, fierce yet always good-humoured Petruchio' went well, and the same critic liked the 'sure and subtle way' in which Pamela Alan showed that 'when she surrendered to this forceful male—she conquered him!' John Neville played Lucentio, Tony Britton Tranio, Newton Blick Baptista, Donald Pleasence Grumio and Gudrun Ure Bianca. Years later, in 'Desert Island Discs' on the

B.B.C., Neville was to include Prokofiev's 'Classical Symphony' among his chosen gramophone records because it reminded him of this production, which used this work as incidental music.

Altogether *The Shrew* finished the Bristol Old Vic innings more successfully than its cricket eleven, who were all out for 53 in a match with Frenchay (who scored 147 for 8 declared) on June 3rd: this despite the picturesque virility of two of the Old Vic batsmen—Donald Pleasence and Hugh Manning—in beards grown for their theatre work. [A.W.]

CHAPTER EIGHT

The Seventh Season
1951 *to* 1952

THE YEAR 1951-2 was a vital one in the history of the Bristol Old Vic. There were three important happenings. The first was an unfortunate one. In the autumn of 1951 Tom Hickson fell ill, and was away for six months. His absence was a definite loss, his genial, welcoming figure in the front of the house having always been so compelling a factor in the building up of a faithful audience. However, during his absence, his assistant, Ivy Bawn, who has been with Tom both at the Princes and at the Royal for nearly thirty years, stepped nobly and ably into the breach. Her handling of the situation won a real respect.

In January 1952 the Bristol Old Vic Company played for the first time at the Old Vic Theatre in London. In the usual crisscross happenings of history, this visit, which was to have far-reaching effects, had come about in a haphazard fashion. It cannot be claimed that the invitation was based on the merits or rising reputation of the company. The simple truth is that in the Waterloo Road there was little short of chaos. In the summer of 1951 there had come the shattering series of resignations, which for a few months had put the Old Vic on to the front page of every newspaper. The convulsions had not yet died down, and although Guthrie was now in charge there was still no stability. In the late autumn of 1951 it was discovered that there would be a two weeks' gap in the planning for the spring and it was hurriedly decided, almost *faute de mieux*, to ask the Bristol Old Vic Company to fill in this fortnight in January.

They followed in after a disastrous production of *A Midsummer Night's Dream*, for which Guthrie had been responsible. Guthrie is a genius who knows no middle course. His productions are either sweeping successes or ghastly failures. There was no doubt about the category to which *The Dream* belonged. Denis Carey's production of *Two Gentlemen of Verona* came into a theatre whose regular audience had dwindled away, whilst its productions could find no favour with the critics. There was an extraordinary atmosphere on that first night. A listless audience, the usual professional first-night theatre-goers, had come without any great expectations; suddenly, during the evening, they found themselves electrified by the gaiety, the poetry, and the deft professionalism of this young company. 'They are enchanting', cried a well-known woman critic to a Bristol official, who was himself on the point of incoherence with pride. The Press, the next day, delighted as always when genuinely able to praise, let themselves go, and from that moment forward the seal was set on the Bristol Old Vic Company. The box office at the Old Vic was overwhelmed. Every theatre management knows the difficulties that can arise in even the best-ordered houses, when there have been no advance bookings or agency arrangements, to pave the way for a sudden success. This was such an occasion at the Old Vic, and every spare member of the staff was conscripted and pushed into the box office to help cope with the flood of postal and telephone requests. In the second fortnight, the house was sold out—this had not happened at the Old Vic since Olivier's days. In a way, the success of the *Two Gentlemen of Verona* has been almost an embarrassment to Bristol, because since then the London Press and public have expected and demanded the best of the company; the second best has not been good enough for them. Not always, in subsequent visits, have the company been able to reach the expected standard.

At the end of March 1952 there came an important change in the legal constitution of the company. Up till then, the Arts Council had been financially responsible for both company and theatre, whilst the conduct of affairs, as we have seen, had been in the hands of the management committee, which, under the chairmanship of Sir Philip Morris, included nominees of the Arts Council, the Old Vic, and latterly those of the Bristol Corporation. In 1951 Mr. W. E. Williams (later Sir William Emrys Williams) had become the secretary-general of the Arts Council, and his immediate policy was to disengage his Council from direct management. It was agreed that, from the beginning of the next financial year (April 1952) the Old Vic Trust should assume sole financial responsibility for the running of the company and the theatre. Like all other associated companies of the Council, they were to receive a yearly grant in accordance with their needs.

The management committee, with its representatives from the three bodies, was to function as before, but the Arts Council, as the lessee, were to remain solely responsible for the upkeep of the eighteenth-century building. Such a charge upon the Council was not unfair, because, as has already been pointed out, the upkeep of a national monument was not a responsibility that a theatre company could reasonably be asked to undertake. Nevertheless, it was agreed that the Bristol Old Vic Company should, in any financially successful year, give two-thirds of its profit to a fund devoted to the maintenance of the building.

It may here be mentioned that, in the ten years that had by this time elapsed since the Arts Council had undertaken the main lease, they had spent on repairs and on repayment of the mortgage a total of about £57,000. Against this sum they had derived about £14,000 in profits from the running of the theatre, and had received £8,000 from the Bristol Corporation, so that their net outlay on the building in those ten years had been about £35,000.

Under these conditions, the Bristol Old Vic Company entered a new phase. For the first time they had become masters in the house. Those members of the staff, including myself, who had been servants of the Council, now became servants of the Old Vic Trust, whilst the beginning of this new order was concurrent with the arrival of Alfred Francis as administrator of the Old Vic Trust.   [C.L.]

Jean Anouilh's *The Traveller Without Luggage*, not previously produced in England, formed on September 3rd, 1951, what the *Western Daily Press* called 'one of the most auspicious openings to a new season the Bristol Old Vic have had'.

It is a dramatic, almost tragic play, on the theme of amnesia. Gaston, a victim of World War I, is released from an asylum to join the family of Renaud, who claim him as a long-lost son and brother. Gaston, with no recollection of his identity himself, sets out to find proof of it, and the evidence he unearths about his past life in the family shakes him so profoundly that he prefers return to the asylum to acknowledging that the vicious boy of the past was actually himself. There is an unexpected dénouement, which *The Times* described as 'surprisingly comic . . . we cannot help feeling that it is the author not the hero who has escaped'; but the detective-story method paid dramatic dividends and the *Western Daily Press* referred to Carey's 'almost flawless pro-

duction of a brilliantly enthralling play'. 'Its chief interest', wrote
The Times, 'springs from the theatrical skill with which it exhibits
in all its facets the horror of a man who cannot escape responsibility
for an evil past.'

John Coe's headlines—'Old Vic in Absorbing Play—Laurence
Payne's Gaston will be remembered'—sum up the general
reaction. Payne's first appearance with the Bristol Old Vic, where
he was to leave glowing memories, was in every sense a triumph:
he 'commands the stage', wrote *The Times*, 'and never once loses
the sympathy of the audience'. 'Laurence Payne's Gaston',
echoed Coe, 'a taut, strained performance—how significant his
pauses were—may well be remembered all the season. It deserves
to be.' 'This magnificent actor is going to make history at the
Royal', added John Bennett.

Coe also found Newton Blick's 'monumental brother' specially
delightful, and Helen Haye as Mme Renaud 'delicately grew',
wrote the *Western Daily Press*, 'into a terrible strength'. Michael
Aldridge was also highly praised as George Renaud, the brother,
to whom he brought sympathy and distinction. This actor, too, was
to do much notable Bristol Old Vic work in the future. Pamela
Alan returned as Valerie Renaud, and John Neville in the small
part of a valet had one effective scene. Newcomers included Sheila
Burrell, who played Juliette, Elaine Wodson (from the Salisbury Arts
Theatre) as the Duchess Dupont-Dufort, and Prunella Scales,
from the London Old Vic School, who had the small part of a
maid. Hutchinson-Scott once again was the Theatre Royal designer.

Miles Malleson's adaptation of Molière's *Le Bourgeois
Gentilhomme*, now entitled *The Prodigious Snob*, evoked the headline: 'Bristol's Old Vic in a Prodigious Hit'. It was a lively version
which had been produced in its rightful place with the opera
Ariadne auf Naxos at the Edinburgh Festival, under Sir Thomas
Beecham, and at Bristol as in Edinburgh Malleson himself, in the
enormous role of the amiable snob, M. Jourdain, had a memorable
success. 'Pathetically comic at one moment and almost tragically
discountenanced the next', in Coe's words, he could swell like a
frog and bleat like a lamb. (J. C. Trewin favoured a more fish-
like metaphor: 'looking like a happy cod with blood-pressure—a
cod resolved to use only the best parts of the ocean'). He is a great
and highly individual comedian the London stage sees too rarely,
in a part or play worthy of his powers, but whose triumphs at

Bristol are reiterated and assured. 'His stay with us has been an inspiration', announced the Bristol Theatre Royal programme.

Carey produced in Scott's gorgeous setting of maroon and gold, with music specially composed by John Hotchkis, and the cast was an interesting one—the Bristol Old Vic School students, Julian Slade and Phyllida Law, making their first Theatre Royal appearance as an anonymous Flunkey and Singer. Aldridge was the Fencing Master and Dorante, Blick the Philosopher, Cook and Mufti, Elaine Wodson Mme. Jourdain, Sheila Burrell Nicole, Pamela Alan Dorimène, and Neville and Prunella Scales the young lovers, Cléante and Lucille. Bob Harris, the dumb boy of *Salad Days*, also put in a first appearance as the Tailor's Assistant.

John Steinbeck's powerful *Of Mice and Men*, which had been played in town just before the war with John Mills as George, made a striking dramatic contrast on October 16th, and was the subject of a programme note worth quoting:

The world we talk about, of food, newspapers, radios, railway journeys, wages, governments, policies and prices, has so catapulted in change that it is already hard to remember what it was like twelve or fourteen years ago, before the war.

Then, John Steinbeck was writing *Of Mice and Men* and *The Grapes of Wrath*. America was grappling with soil erosion, starvation and restless, angry, itinerant farm workers. Much of the anger and bitterness was thrusting forth into America's dramatic literature and some of the strongest and bitterest plays of the period emerged. Strangely enough, though he writes perhaps even more strongly than any of his contemporaries, in Steinbeck there is neither anger nor bitterness. A profound pity, perhaps, for men, for the straits they get themselves into, a profound admiration for the greatness that is in them at their most simple and stern, a deep understanding of their wilfulness, grasp and greed, but more patently than all these a poet's feeling and hurt, in the vision of all men's struggles with the imponderable forces of life and circumstances against which, with so little, they fight so courageously.

It is this penetration of vision in prose and dialogue as sensitive as any poet's verse, that lifts Steinbeck's novels and plays above the work of his many fine American contemporaries. It is found at its finest in *Of Mice and Men*, the story of two

men, vagrant in the search for work, the one, of the simplicity
of less than a child, dependent upon the protecting affection and
courage of the other.

It was a fine production which in Coe's words 'captures the
poetry of Steinbeck's writing and wrings compassion from us with
as little effort as the tousled Lennie strangles dumb animals'.
Nevertheless, Laurence Payne was not entirely suited to the
American idiom of George, and according to Dennis Bushell 'it
was left to John Neville to surmount that barrier with ease and give
very nearly the best performance. Not only does Mr. Neville's
Slim thoroughly convince, it is also one of the outstanding studies
of the season so far'. The character part of the young but mature
foreman was in fact one which Neville found particularly congenial—'a lovely part'—and Michael Aldridge was outstanding
as the huge and tragically simple Lennie. Sheila Burrell played
Curly's Wife, the part enacted by the pre-war blonde bombshell,
Claire Luce, in London. The splendid sets of Patrick Robertson
had striking atmosphere and did much to establish his talent.

Hugh Hunt returned on November 6th, 1951, with a production
of *Love's Labour's Lost*, the comedy which had marked his début
as Director of the London Old Vic at the New Theatre in 1949,
and was still remembered for its enchantment. Hutchinson-Scott
composed 'three pictures of dewy, fragile loveliness' and the
costumes of Payne as Berowne and Yvonne Coulette as Katharine;
otherwise the costumes were those by Berkeley Sutcliffe used by
the London Old Vic, and the production itself, with its mingled
gaiety and lyricism, elegance and final falling leaves, echoed the
London one closely. Michael Aldridge's Armado was possibly
the outstanding performance (he had played Ferdinand of
Navarre in Hunt's London production)—Coe wrote of its 'extreme
pity' and called it 'beautifully imaginative', while Bushell thought
'Michael Aldridge emerges brilliantly as Armado and almost
succeeds in humanising a type'. But with Payne as Berowne (he
had already played it with the Old Vic Company resident at
Liverpool during the war), Sheila Burrell as Rosaline, Pamela
Alan as Princess of France, Yvonne Coulette (Carey's wife) in
her first Bristol Old Vic part as Katharine, and Blick as Holofernes
the company was not a mean Shakespearian one. Among the lesser-
knowns Slade appeared as the Messenger Mercade, Christopher

Burgess (later to do small parts at the London Old Vic) as Sir Nathaniel and William Eedle, a former Bristol student, as Costard.

John Neville, the Berowne of a later London Old Vic production, played Ferdinand, King of Navarre (Michael Redgrave had played the same two parts, in the same order, for the Old Vic during his career), and John Coe distinguished himself as a prophet: 'I should say John Neville has written his own introduction to the Old Vic in London on the strength of his Navarre in this play.'

Venus Observed on November 27th brought the Bristol Old Vic its second Fry play. 'It is strange to think', meditated the programme note, 'that the theme is the same as that of *Of Mice and Men*—Loneliness—though the treatment could hardly be more different.' Its loneliness is the loneliness of autumn, the sere, and though the Duke of Altair is lightly observed his story is touched with a wry melancholy—yellow leaf after the fresh, green, abundant spring of *The Lady's Not for Burning*. Payne had already played the part at the Guildford Repertory and had also acted Thomas Mendip for the Salisbury Arts Theatre: he fell naturally into the Fry idiom and his arresting, dark face with its Slavonic cheekbones had the right cast of intelligence and civilised irony. 'What does it matter if the weight of years sits too lightly on the shoulders of Laurence Payne', challenged Dennis Bushell, 'so long as he gives us the poetic gleam, the dreams, the delicate perception and smooth refinement of this Duke?'

Sheila Burrell's Perpetua, he added, 'has a loveliness which seems distinct from the art of Fry. A remarkably rich performance'. Pamela Alan was the intense fire-raiser, Rosabel, John Neville (lover of Fry's work) the gently reticent son Edgar, Newton Blick the delightfully dishonest and loyal Reedbeck, Elaine Wodson Jessie Dill and Yvonne Coulette Hilda Taylor-Snell. Aldridge and Burgess provided the comic relief as the quarrelsome Captain Fox Reddleman and Bates, the reformed-burglar footman, and Bushell admired Paul Eddington's 'cameo of preciseness'. 'Framed in Hutchinson-Scott's setting, this production is a living vision of delight.'

Once again V. C. Clinton-Baddeley provided the pantomime—*Jack and the Beanstalk*, with music by Gavin Gordon. It was notable for its folk-style melodies—'Rosemary for Remembrance', 'Where there's a will there's a way', 'The British Batsman'—and the introduction of a helicopter, and Coe (of the *Evening Post*) noted 'the *Evening Post* scholarship winner, Phyllida Law, who with another pupil, Elizabeth West, has brought the peregrinations of Daisy, the cow, to an astonishingly high level of precision and timing'. Elizabeth West, a dancer-actress also trained in the Bristol School, was later to arrange the dances for *Salad Days* and *The Duenna*, in which she also danced most engagingly.

Blick was the Dame, Aldridge 'Sir Bertram Bounder', Elaine Wodson Fairy Moonbeam and Pamela Alan again Principal Boy. The charming soprano, Eleanor Drew, for so long the heroine of *Salad Days*, appeared with the company for the first time as the heroine, Chloe. Edward Stanley produced, with settings by Kenneth Lawson and costumes by Peggy Lancaster.

Julian Slade first appeared as composer with the incidental music for *Two Gentlemen of Verona*, first produced for two weeks on February 4th, 1952, and immediately transferred with great success for a short season at the London Old Vic. Designed in the style of a Renaissance masque by Hutchinson-Scott, who used metal, gauze and sheet tin for his scenery (the texture, we were assured, 'lends itself to the decorative quality of the play'), the freshness and spellbinding quality of the production was much remarked upon. 'The Old Vic takes it at a brisk pace', wrote Coe, 'and once again makes the poetry ring. No one makes it ring more than John Neville, who plays the vigorous and ardent Valentine with complete authority.' 'The curtains', wrote the *Western Daily Press*, 'rise on a song, in a setting of scalloped-edged pillars and plush-walls with lights flickering down the backcloth like falling snow' (it was a permanent setting, with changes of lighting only to convey change of place and atmosphere).

In London, Stephen Williams admired its 'shining vitality' and proclaimed it 'as charming an entertainment as any in London' (he also longed to see the Julia, Pamela Alan, as Rosalind). 'That rarely-staged comedy, the *Two Gentlemen of Verona*, is notable for at least two things—it contains that lovely lyric "Who is Silvia?" and the best part ever written for a dog', wrote A. E. Wilson, and he thought the Crab showed 'human and intelligent understanding in every wag of his tail'. The dog was Michael Aldridge's, and set a precedent by failing, in spite of his brilliant talents, to divert attention wholly from his master Launce, in which part Aldridge scored an outstanding success—appealing, brilliant and pathetic were among the epithets he inspired. Newton Blick's Speed, too, was not overlooked: 'What Speed lacks in lines he makes up for in the ripe eloquence of Newton Blick's face', wrote Cecil Wilson. Harold Hobson (who thought this the 'most enchanted evening we have had south of the river' since the Old Vic left the West End), found in Laurence Payne's Proteus 'the disturbing attractiveness of a Sicilian bandit with an uneasy conscience', and John Neville as Valentine duly set London buzzing for the first time. 'John Neville, looking rather like the young Mr. Gielgud, brings to his wooing the hint of ease and aristocracy which is called for by comedy of this kind', wrote *The Times*, and Richard Findlater was prophetic: 'Mr. Neville has, I am sure, a starry future. He has charm, good looks, poise, fluency and style—an overworked term, but a rare quality.'

Gudrun Ure returned to play Silvia, and two interesting new names were John Warner as Thurio and William Squire as the Duke of Milan. Both were to do good work later for the London Old Vic. Squire had already appeared as Oberon, Laertes and Ulysses at Stratford-on-Avon, and at the Birmingham Repertory; but Warner and Eleanor Drew (here an anonymous Singer) could hardly have anticipated during this production their long love-tryst in *Salad Days*. Slade himself composed nine songs for the production—as many as possible with Shakespearian lyrics and in Elizabethan *pastiche*, with a twenty-year-old guitarist, Mildred Clary, as accompanist.

Two Gentlemen of Verona had been produced at the Bristol Theatre Royal only once before in the past two hundred years— by Macready in 1822, when it ended incongruously but lavishly with 'a gorgeous display of Cleopatra's galley'. The Bristol Old Vic revival took an equal, if less spectacular, place in history, and reminded us that Dr. Johnson's estimate of its 'eminently beautiful' lines of poetry was not without foundation.

> O, how this spring of love resembleth
> The uncertain glory of an April day ...

'A charming and wilful comedy', as Denis Carey, its producer, described it.

The revival of the French farce of *An Italian Straw Hat*, by Labiche and Marc-Michel, which followed on March 4th, 1952, also attracted London Old Vic attention (it was produced in the

Desmond Tripp

The Lady's Not for Burning (Christopher Fry), 1950. John Phillips
(right) as Thomas Mendip and John Neville as Richard.

ABOVE: *The Traveller Without Luggage* (Anouilh), 1951. Laurence Payne as Gaston and Sheila Burrell as Juliette.

BELOW: *Love's Labour's Lost*, 1951. Production by Hugh Hunt. Settings and costumes by Hutchinson-Scott.

Both photos by Desmond Tripp

ABOVE: *Of Mice and Men* (John Steinbeck), 1951. Setting by Patrick Robertson with Laurence Payne (George) and Michael Aldridge (Lennie).

BELOW: *The Love of Four Colonels* (Peter Ustinov), 1952. L. *to* R. George Hagan (Frappot), Arthur Howard (Rinder-Sparrow), Newton Blick (Breitenspiegel) and Michael Aldridge (Ikonenko).

Both photos by Desmond Tripp

ABOVE: *The Wild Duck* (Ibsen), 1953. L. *to* R. Dorothy Reynolds (Gina), Maureen Quinney (Hedvig), Robert Eddison (Hjalmar Ekdal), John Neville (Gregers Werle).

BELOW: *Love for Love* (Congreve), 1953. L. *to* R. Maxine Audley (Mrs. Foresight), Robert Cartland (Scandal), Lee Montague (Ben), Dorothy Reynolds (Mrs. Frail).

Waterloo Road the following season, with several of the Bristol cast). It had been the famous subject of a René Clair film and the present adaptation by Thomas Walton fitted Bristol's mood better than London's. Carey produced spiritedly (he included a Can-Can) with sets by Joyce Hammond and costumes by Rosemary Vercoe, and William Squire as the bride's deaf uncle, Blick as her father, John Warner as the elderly piano-playing 'beau' Achille and Payne as Fadinard, the dapper and harassed bridegroom, were to repeat their expert performances with the London Vic Company. In Bristol Patricia Blyton played the bride, Pamela Alan the milliner, Clara, Michael Aldridge M. Beaujolais and Norman Tyrrell the senile shopwalker, Tardiveau, in which Paul Rogers was to make such a triumph (immediately preceding his stardom as Shylock) in the London production.

T. S. Eliot's *Family Reunion*, on March 25th, could hardly have been a more profound contrast. First produced before the war at the Westminster Theatre, with Michael Redgrave as the Fury-pursued Harry, Lord Monchensey, it was written before Eliot's experiments in economic prose-style dramatic verse, and though its language sometimes flames its Greek tragedy parallels and religious implications do not leap easily to all understandings. An imaginative production by Peter Brook at the Phoenix Theatre in 1956, with a superb cast headed by Sybil Thorndike, Gwen Ffrangcon-Davies and Paul Scofield, has shown the mystic cogency and drama of the play to be not only ingrained but lucid: it is a play of spiritual self-recognition, with Harry's Erinyes of guilt turning into the Eumenides, or 'bright angels', of enlightenment with his realisation, through Agatha, the aunt who loves him and knows his background, that his torment springs from an inner spiritual need, a way of life and service which eliminates problems, once recognised.

It is a difficult play to do well and the chorus of the aunts and uncles—uncomprehending yet fearful in their prosaic world—defeats most producers. Yet there are fine moments and fine parts, and the Bristol production did not wholly fail. Carey suggested the Eumenides only by a bright light in the sky outside the windows, and when speaking their secret thoughts 'the characters', wrote the *Western Daily Press*, 'freeze into complete immobility, so that they appear almost to become two-dimensional'. The production, wrote T. C. Worsley in the *New Statesman and Nation*, was 'so sure of itself and so compelling that it might make Mr. Eliot modify some of the self-criticism he addressed to his own play in a recent lecture. Stillness is the keynote of the production, and it comes in good time to remind us that the fashionable modern bustle and movement ("all this is far too static. You must move *somewhere* on that line") is, as the French recently showed us, by no means the most effective for poetic drama'.

Beatrix Lehmann came as guest artist to play Amy: 'Miss Lehmann's Dowager is so powerfully intense that every word, almost every intake of breath, is like the crack of doom', wrote John Coe, and the *Western Daily Press* referred to her 'snapping and barking her words, and presenting a cold, bleak, rigid and distant figure'. An interesting newcomer played Agatha: Dorothy Reynolds, later part-author of *Salad Days* and a Bristol Old Vic actress of range and distinction. The mystic qualities of Agatha did not entirely suit her, but her 'statuesque poise' was commented on. The Harry was Laurence Payne, always good in the haunted and neurotically intense. Elaine Wodson and another excellent newcomer, Margot Van Der Burgh, were the two aunts, Aldridge and Blick the uncles, Pamela Alan Mary, the younger woman of the household, and William Squire Dr. Warburton.

The Love of Four Colonels brought Bristol its first Peter Ustinov play, and another highly original production. Ustinov's programme note is perhaps the best comment on the play:

> A playwright who is also an actor can be bound by neither literature nor technique; he must exploit an amalgam of both . . . there must also exist a certain malaise which springs from a contemporary artist's consciousness that we live in a period without a style. . . . The triumph of men such as Hindemith, Stravinsky, Anouilh and Picasso is that they have discovered a personal style, but while they exert a justified influence, it does |not mean that they have discovered a style for anybody else.
>
> *Love of Four Colonels* is a play designed by an actor for actors . . . the words are, on the surface, the road-signs for an evening of improvisation. They are also the bricks with which an edifice of serious purpose is constructed.
>
> I deem it the function of the dramatist to ask questions, not to answer them. Without the ever-present doubts of the human

animal, there is no tragedy and not much comedy. Convictions are unconvincing. And why? Because the theatre is the play-ground of characters who lend their conflicting viewpoints to their creator. . . . There is a message in the very inability of the characters to agree, and there is a message in their un-deniable affection for each other at the end. Apart from that, I chose to remain silent about my intentions. That is the business of my critics, by which I mean my audience.

All I will say in conclusion is that this is a comedy to be enjoyed at the time and thought about later. Thus it is a comedy in which the audience must work as hard as the actors. It is the duty of the actors, God bless them, to make it seem as though the audience has no work to do at all.

The four colonels, Render-Sparrow, Breitenspiegel, Frappot and Ikonenko were played by Arthur Howard (brother to Leslie Howard), Newton Blick, George Hagan and Michael Aldridge; Squire and Yvonne Coulette were Two Miserable Immortals; and Pamela Alan the Beauty. Squire in the Ustinov part, wrote the *Western Daily Press*, 'played with abundant versatility . . . an actor so light-footed that he gives the impression of walking on air. His eyes and gestures have a devil in them, sometimes a wicked devil, sometimes a humorous one, and sometimes a suggestively perverse one'. Pamela Alan was also much praised for her 'keen powers of mimicry'. It was Hagan's first appearance with the company. He had been a fine Bastard in *King John* with the London Old Vic early in the war, but had been rather lost sight of since his service in the Royal Air Force which followed.

The producer, unexpectedly, was Laurence Payne. 'Laurence Payne takes his leave of the Bristol Old Vic company with a performance as auspicious as when he made his first appearance at the beginning of the season', wrote the *Western Daily Press*. 'But his role has changed. He came as an actor to give a beautifully sensitive and moving portrayal of an amnesia victim in a play from the modern French school, and he departs by directing with skill and wit an ultra-modern pantomime from the pen of one of England's foremost actor-dramatists.'

Macbeth, on May 6th, 1952, was Aldridge's only considerable failure with the company. He was not an actor scaled to the part—though he had played Othello in the Nottingham Repertory production at the London St. James's Theatre in 1948—but one critic thought he grew in stature as the play proceeded: 'a lowering figure but with a grisly look', speaking his verse 'passionately and sensibly'. His voice was described as too tender in quality, though he had intelligent and sympathetic touches. It was not enough, although the production, opening with a thunderous roll of drums, caught what was described as 'a granite-like atmosphere of grim and forbidding gloom'. Hutchinson-Scott set the play between permanent battlements raised to frame an inner picture, with changing colours, and Carey made much use of pools and shafts of light. Pamela Alan had greater success as Lady Macbeth—an 'impressive, steely performance'—'a full-blooded, fiery, she-cat of a Lady Macbeth'—and Squire was a noble Banquo. Hagan stayed on to play Macduff (years before at Stratford he had been a memorable Ross), and Blick was the inevitable Porter.

John Whiting's *A Penny For a Song* was a comedy of distinction —almost an extravaganza—set in the time of the Napoleonic Wars, when England formed its first Home Guard and hourly awaited invasion. One could not anticipate here the controversial *Saint's Day* which was to split the theatre like an atom (and cause almost as great an explosion), nor the fine, intellectual contemporary play, *Marching Song*, which was to be one of the Bristol Old Vic's most memorable productions in the 1954-5 season; but the original tone of the play made its mark and Bushell praised Carey's production 'which tumbles about in fun, but also captures the more elusive spirit of this delicate piece'.

Carey himself brought the atmosphere of the play to life in one of his voluminous programme notes: '*A Penny For a Song* breathes the peaceful air of a hot summer's day in the country. Peaceful! No, that is hardly the word. For cannon-balls roll, trumpets sound, fires blaze. Rumours of invasion are rife, and someone looking perilously like Napoleon Bonaparte emerges dishevelled, but triumphant, from the dark recesses of a well. . . . *All the characters have a unique capacity for joy*. Whether it be Lamprett at his fire engine, or Timothy in his fantastic plans to repel the invasion, or Hester with her band of Amazons. . . .' (It is worth noting Whiting based the activities of his characters on contemporary reports—there was actually an Amazon Corps formed in Yorkshire!—and that his father was stationed in Bath with the Wiltshire Regiment in the 1920s: a professional military home background which must have influenced both this play and *Marching Song*, in widely different ways.)

Coe thought Michael Aldridge, as Hallam Matthews, gave the best performance (it was a consolation, doubtless, after Macbeth), but Squire as Sir Timothy Bellboys and Blick as Lamprett Bellboys brilliantly supported. Dorothy Reynolds played Hester Bellboys and Carol Marsh, a Rank film starlet, appeared with the company for the first time as Dorcas. Hutchinson-Scott designed a garden scene rising in formal terraces which was described as a horticultural problem for the stage staff and Nat Brenner.

The season ended with a week's revival of *Two Gentlemen of Verona* beginning on June 29th, and on July 3rd the production returned to the London Old Vic for three weeks—a real accolade for the Bristol branch. [A.W.]

CHAPTER NINE

The Eighth Season
1952 *to* 1953

DENIS CAREY was now at the height of his powers. He had established around him a more or less permanent company, and although the individual members might change from time to time—flit to London for film or television, and then return again —the pattern remained the same. John Neville, Newton Blick, Dorothy Reynolds, Pamela Alan, Michael Aldridge, Yvonne Coulette, Robert Cartland, James Cairncross, were the Carey-ites. Today they form as definite a group in the London theatre as do the offshoots of the St. Denis School. It is from their ranks that the many recruits to the ever-changing cast of the phenomenal London run of *Salad Days* have been quite naturally drawn. But there was more to it than a group devoted to their leader. Carey believed in the existence of the team as an essential part of the corporate theatre. It was his belief that the greatest contribution such a group could make would be in the creation and production of its own plays. It was his determination and his enthusiasm that egged on Dorothy Reynolds, James Cairncross and the brilliant lad Julian Slade to the writing and composing of *Christmas in King Street*. The secret of this play, its successor in the following year, *The Merry Gentleman*, and finally *Salad Days*, is that all three were written by members of the company, for the company, around the known characteristics of the company, under the inspiration of a man who knew how to extract the best from each ingredient.

There were other factors at work making for success, and throughout Carey was aided by his faithful henchman, Nat Brenner. In the summer of 1952 Edward Stanley, who had been for two years both director of the school and assistant manager to Carey, felt that all his energies were now needed by the School, and he was replaced in the company by Nat Brenner, who, however, took the title of production manager. Brenner had been stage manager at Coventry, immediately after the war, when Carey had been an acting member of the Midland Theatre Company. Together they had gone to Salisbury, and from Salisbury to Bristol. Now, with Brenner leaving his dark little room behind-stage (once Mrs. Siddons's dressing-room) and sharing a desk in Carey's office, there began a close collaboration, and a communion of two similar minds, from which sprang most of the fruitful work of the next two years.

The School was at that time in the doldrums. Six years in a confined space over a greengrocer's store could not be conducive to the best work, and it says much for Stanley that he was able to turn out such good material—of which shining examples are Phyllida Law, Bob Harris and Elizabeth Charnley, today one of the leading stage directors in London. The search for new premises went on, but in a Bristol barely recovered from the blitz there was no free space, and, even if there had been, there was no money in the Bristol Old Vic coffers to acquire it. Had it not been for the help of the University, which proffered both accommodation and funds, the struggle of maintaining the school would have been impossible.

Meanwhile the company progressed in importance, with regular visits to the London Old Vic, but its great moment came when an invitation arrived to represent the British Theatre at the International Festival at Zürich. The London Old Vic had played there in the three previous summers, and it was at the instigation of the British Council that the invitation for June 1953 was extended to Bristol. The company took their Coronation production of *Henry the Fifth* and flew from London Airport to Zürich. It was five days of packed excitement for the youngsters—some of them had never been out of England before, and many of them had never flown before. The hospitality and warmth of the Swiss was amazing, and the reception of *Henry the Fifth* was rapturous. The Press also was most cordial and appreciative, but it has to be recorded with regret that the performance given by all in Zürich—and especially by John Neville—was far more satisfying and far more complete than anything that had been seen in the previous three weeks in Bristol, or was to be seen during the following fortnight in London. John Coe accompanied the company, and sent back his dispatches by special airmail, so that during the week of the company's absence about twenty columns of news and photos appeared in the *Bristol Evening Post*. The only one factor that damped the company's ardour was the weather. It began to rain from the moment that the aircraft dipped down at Zürich, and it rained incessantly during the visit. A luncheon given by the British Council in a pavilion on the lake was accompanied by a mountain storm, and the rain battering on the glass walls had the sound of machine-gun fire. It was with a wry smile that the company learned on their return to London that the week of their absence had provided the only heat-wave so far that summer.

This eighth season, incidentally, was, in accordance with the new arrangements, the first under the full management of the Old Vic Trust. When the change-over had been mooted in the spring of 1952, I had attended a meeting of the Old Vic Trust, and warned them that they must anticipate a loss of £4,000 on the running of the company, which must be offset by grants from the Arts Council. The figures for the financial year 1952-3 proved to be the second best in the whole history of the company. Instead of the predicted loss, the profits totalled almost £4,000. Under the new agreement, two-thirds of this profit was handed over to the Arts Council Reserve Fund for the maintenance of the building.   [C.L.]

Carey's third season opened on September 1st, 1952, with a return to Fry and Anouilh: this double being achieved, of course, with the comedy-fantasy *Ring Round the Moon*, the delightful play about twins of opposite character, a Cinderella-like ballerina, and a formidable eccentric duchess which had charmed audiences in town with Paul Scofield, Claire Bloom and Margaret Rutherford in the leading parts.

John Neville had been absent from several plays at the end of the previous season, when he had been in Denmark taking part in TV films of Hans Andersen's stories. He had returned for the revival of *Two Gentlemen of Verona* and now made a welcome re-appearance as Hugo and Frederic, the twins. Having much of Scofield's distinguished good looks and elegance he fitted the parts well and was highly praised for his differentiation of the characters. A review in *The Stage* demurred on this, but its balanced judgment is interesting now: 'a good steadfast actor of principle and profile, both set too firmly to allow wide enough range of expression for these twins of such different personality. His Hugo is not almost a devil, he is not even quite a devil, while Frederic, rather implacably gauche, is nowhere near a thousand times as nice. But Mr. Neville has great ability and with such looks, such romantic resonance, such sincerity, he can hardly avoid being a major success this season'.

Carol Marsh also returned to play the heroine, Isabelle,[1] with 'refreshing charm and pointed delivery', and Dorothy Reynolds to play the Duchess: 'an eccentric body with a voice like the sound of tearing calico', as described by Dennis Bushell. Elaine Wodson as the companion Capulat, Margot Van Der Burgh as the young spitfire Diana Messerschmann and Kenneth Mackintosh as 'Joshua, a crumbling butler', were others who had played before with the Bristol Old Vic. The newcomers included Robert Cartland in Cecil Trouncer's part of the rich eccentric Messerschmann, Richard Wordsworth as the lepidopterist (this fair, attractive young actor was to specialise in senile parts later with Gielgud), Pauline Jameson (also a player in Gielgud's Coronation season at the Lyric, Hammersmith) as Lady India, Audrey Noble as Isabelle's mother, and Richard Gale (later of the London Old Vic) as Patric Bombelles. Audrey Noble was a Bristol-born actress who the following season appeared with the Birmingham Repertory as Clytemnestra in Euripides' *Iphigenia in Aulis* and in other parts.

One of the enchantments of the London production had been Oliver Messel's crystal-palace décor and wittily mixed-period costumes. Hutchinson-Scott did the Bristol designs along similar lines, and Denis Carey produced. Nat Brenner, following good service as Stage Director, this season replaced Edward Stanley as Production Manager. His grasp of stage lighting was to add distinction to many productions in the future, and his production of Lorca's *Blood Wedding* for the Bristol Old Vic School students in 1955 was to impress the professional company greatly.

Measure for Measure on September 30th was produced by Basil Coleman, who had been responsible for several London opera productions, including Benjamin Britten's *Billy Budd* at Covent Garden. The play had not been performed in Bristol since 1813, and evoked startling difference of opinion in the local press. It was, according to Dennis Bushell in the *Evening World*, a 'plain and unvarnished production, a heavy task beyond the capabilities of the present company'. John Coe in the *Evening Post*, contrariwise, praised the 'imaginative treatment' of the producer

---

[1] Anouilh's master, Giraudoux, in *Intermezzo* (played later in Bristol as *The Enchanted*), also has an enchanting heroine of this name.

and the 'authoritative playing of a strong Bristol Old Vic company'. 'There are times when Isabella's first scene with Angelo has the atmosphere of the exam. room', snapped Bushell. 'Warmth and ardency' wrote the *Western Daily Press* of Margot Van Der Burgh's playing of the same character. Neville's 'rant at the end of the third act' was 'like a demon king in pantomime' (Bushell). Neville 'treats us to ranges of his golden voice hitherto unsounded' (*Western Daily Press*). 'John Neville's Duke is so good that it almost unbalances the production'! (Coe).

As for Robert Eddison, who returned to play the difficult but psychologically fascinating part of Angelo, his lot was less 'snowbroth' than snowball between the critics. To Bushell he revealed his hand too soon: 'he is the hypocritical lecher before the austerity of the character can be established. . . . The lack of contrast between the outer and the inner Angelo robs the play of much of its emphasis before it has progressed very far'. 'No snowbroth —no congealed ice' was the summing-up. But 'Eddison finds both Angelo's blood of snowbroth and his conscience' contradicted the *Western Daily Press* flatly, and to Coe he was 'capital'—'a symbol of incorruptibility'.

Eddison's response to this conflict (he is a man of reading and intelligence) was doubtless resigned if not actually amused. Coleman himself had already set out his views on the play, and many will agree with him that, like most of these later-phase plays of Shakespeare, including the so-called 'romances'—*The Winter's Tale, The Tempest*—*Measure for Measure* is in some sense a symbolic play, probing the relationship of divinity and human morality; the final synthesis of ideas and experience in a man whose life was already drawing to its close, and to whom in his maturity the psychological and metaphysical problem meant more than rationality of plot and the actual 'tools' of his dramatic trade. 'I believe', wrote Coleman, 'it is about different forms of Justice—Earthly Justice which is imposed by our laws and upheld in our courts, and the far greater and mysterious Divine Justice.'

Richard Wordsworth's Lucio was an undisputed success— 'like a shaft of sunlight in a dark vault', wrote Bushell, suddenly unsoured. It is a character, indeed, grateful to play, and the good actor with a vein of irony and flash of personality not infrequently runs away with the stage notices in it. Another Richard, the attractive, well-spoken Gale, played Claudio—a part of considerable opportunity if the young actor cast for it is experienced and virile enough not to fall into the trap of neurotic fear and self-pity (it has some splendid lines of poetry, almost Donne-like on death). James Cairncross was the Pompey, Dorothy Reynolds the Mistress Overdone, Robert Cartland the Escalus and Julian Slade a First Gentleman.

In *She Stoops to Conquer* Coleman was on safer ground, and his production was described as having 'a touch of featheriness in its romance and a sweep of the down-to-earth in its rusticity'. The introduction of the players to Julian Slade music was commented on, and John Neville's Young Marlow was a neat and humorous successor to his Charles Surface. Charles Radclyffe in the *Bath Critic* thought it 'started off with all the grace in the world and ended a trifle short of wind'; but for another critic 'John Neville's look of a deflated codfish during his first tremulous encounter as Young Marlow with an amused Miss Hardcastle' would stay long in the memory. Wordsworth was the Tony Lumpkin, and Radclyffe's criticism that it was 'obviously the work of an actor who is essentially urban rather than rural in all he does' was probably just. Kenneth Mackintosh played Mr. Hardcastle, Dorothy Reynolds Mrs. Hardcastle, Pauline Jameson Kate, Margot Van Der Burgh Constance Neville, and James Cairncross Hastings. Joyce Hammond designed.

The Bridge, a new play by Lionel Shapiro, on November 11th, 1952, was produced by arrangement with Henry Sherek, who had an interest in it. Based on Shapiro's own best-selling novel, *Journey Into Night*, it was a good play with a serious theme—the rescue of a Czech scientist from his Communist-dominated country by an American tycoon, completely honest in his way, who banks on his scientific co-operation in his own oil problems, but finds the scientist strangely disillusioned and still torn in loyalties on his emergence into the Western world. The first act, at a small frontier hotel where the scientist is expected but fails to appear, has a fine tension, and the atmosphere of the bridge outside, where some of the action takes place and on which we are conscious of the presence of the 'enemy', is dramatically 'placed'. There is much robust argument and conflict of will, perhaps a trifle too much sex laid on in the form of the tiresome blonde mistress of an adventurer concerned in the rescue, and a general anticipation of some powerfully delineated theme which does not quite come to pass. The scientist's scruples, when he appears, are psychologically interesting yet not quite plausibly enough activated, and his suicide does not therefore carry the full tragic conviction. Nor is the mysterious figure on the bridge— a state minister who had been the scientist's favourite pupil, and now seeks by persuasion to re-win him for his Communist country —very credibly or deeply drawn. One would like to know more about what 'makes him tick', and perhaps it is a character that needs the novelist's space for analysis.

Nevertheless, the play, produced by Carey with settings by Hutchinson-Scott, was a gallant grapple with an essentially contemporary theme, 'created', as Shapiro himself wrote, 'out of a natural reaction to the world we live in'; and Douglas Campbell and James Cairncross, as the American and the scientist, 'missed no chance of subtly filling out their characters in every dimension', wrote Gerard Fay in the *Manchester Guardian*. Robert Cartland's Hungarian adventurer was an equal success. 'Mr. Shapiro, with magical assistance from the actor Robert Cartland, has created in the infuriating extravert, Alexandrow, who rescues the Professor, a vital character who seems bound sooner or later to be played by Orson Welles in a film', wrote the critic of the magazine *Theatre*, and Charles Radclyffe was still more emphatic: 'Robert Cartland's voluble Hungarian scientist-snatcher will get no praise from me simply because I am tired of praising Mr. Cartland. With his latest creation he has established himself as the most valuable and versatile actor in the present Bristol company.'

Pauline Jameson gave a tense performance as the scientist's worried daughter Moussia Karlene, and Georgina Cookson, wrote W. A. Darlington in the *Daily Telegraph*, 'is a dumb blonde so much to the life that it was a recurrent astonishment to find that she could speak at all'. Neville played the good role of an intelligent young journalist in pursuit of a 'story'—nominally the hero—and Kenneth Mackintosh the local gendarme, Albert, an elderly busybody of character.

Ben Jonson's *The Alchemist* had been a fairly successful Old Vic production at the New Theatre, with Ralph Richardson as Face, George Relph as Subtle and Alec Guinness as Abel Drugger —the part 'written up' for Garrick into starry possibilities Jonson never thought of. It is an acid comedy of human gullibility—the alchemist of Jacobean times has many different successors in the modern world, extracting money from the credulous, from the fake medium to (some would tartly add) the psychiatrist, and the comic sting is by no means therefore a purely period one. Carey's production was 'a rapid series of swiftly established, vivid impressions', wrote Bushell, who also listed the characters and their players with an equally vivid pen: 'the dancing, black wisp with a chuckle like crackling paper that James Cairncross makes of Subtle; the Cockney cunning of John Neville's Face; Robert Cartland puffed out with plum-coloured velvet and cutting an absurd caper as Sir Epicure Mammon; the "smock rampant" Pauline Jameson makes of Doll Common; and the palsied crow—or a spectre from St. Trinian's cupboard, if you like—that Peter Nicholls conjures out of the sable-clad Ananias'. *The Stage* also drew one piquant picture: 'John Neville, an actor of breeding, here acquires ingratiating adenoids and the common touch.'

Richard Burrell, a young actor trained in the Old Vic School under St. Denis, Byam Shaw and Devine, and brother to Sheila, played Abel Drugger, with Dorothy Reynolds as the marriageable widow, Dame Pliant, played so startlingly by Margaret Leighton in London. Pat Robertson designed.

Christmas in King Street on December 24th, 1952, made Bristol Old Vic history. It was Julian Slade's first 'musical', devised specially for the company by Dorothy Reynolds, James Cairncross and Slade himself, although ideas, as in later shows, were subject to many exterior suggestions and Carey's own influence was considerable. 'The ingredients were brought together, after the rest of the day's work was done, in moments snatched from sleep and time', he wrote. 'Everyone had a hand in the stirring, as is only right on these occasions.'

It was a local story, as the title suggests, based on a play-within-a-play construction, and its success was immediate, inquiries regarding the recording of the music being made before the end of the run. Slade himself was invited to compose the music for *The Merchant of Venice* at Stratford-on-Avon.

'The long-awaited, much-debated, oft-requested, hitherto untested Bristol Old Vic Company revue has arrived in an evening of wit, ingenuity and bubbling spirits', wrote the *Western Daily Press*. 'Up to now', wrote Coe, 'we have known Julian Slade as a composer of tinkling music incidental to some of the Old Vic's classical revivals. On this occasion he emerges as a writer of popular

tunes that with a little encouragement from the public could
easily become hit ones. His "Mermaid Scales", for example, has
remained with me throughout Christmas. In the same class, too,
is "Take Me Back to the Ocean". To say that Mr. Slade is more
than half the show is to state no less than the truth.'

Dorothy Reynolds distinguished herself in the Theatre Royal
sequence as the Ghost of Sarah Siddons, with James Cairncross as
the Producer and Norman Rossington the Author of the play. In
the play, Cairncross doubled Mr. Room and Neptune, Reynolds
was Mrs. Room, and Gwen Cherrell, a charming actress from
repertory (and a later Old Vic Olivia, Celia and Doll Tearsheet),
was the heroine. 'Her Victoria is serenely demure yet full of a warm,
smiling quality that, with an economy of gesture, manages to
irradiate the stage', wrote Coe. Her duet with John Neville was
described as 'enchantingly sung with a lingering air'. Neville was
a policeman hero (P.C. Tom Blenkinsop) whose adventures
included a pursuit of criminals who had stolen a Bristol statue of
Queen Victoria, Cartland as a suffragette chained himself to
Neptune in the cause of female emancipation, and Richard
Burrell and Peter Bryant (both newcomers in the previous play)
were suitors suitably droll and boisterously inconsequential. Bob
Harris, the company's Assistant Stage Manager, mimed a dumb
part as in the later *Salad Days*, and Elizabeth West arranged the
dances.

It was Hutchinson-Scott's last play as resident designer (like
Slade he had been engaged for the Stratford *Merchant of Venice*).
His successor was Patrick Robertson, who had already done good
work and at thirty deserved his position. Pauline Jameson also
now left, Maxine Audley succeeding her in the company. David
Bird, Lee Montague, Andrée Melly (who had understudied Claire
Bloom as Juliet at the Old Vic) and Maureen Quinney (Phebe in
the Stratford *As You Like It*) were other newcomers for the spring
half of the season. Both Montague and Maureen Quinney, like
Burrell, had been students of the London Old Vic School.

Congreve's *Love for Love*, on January 23rd, 1953, was a robust
and stylish play selection, which did not wholly match up in
production. Carey produced for speed and stage 'business', but
the general verdict was that the first act fell flatly and the play
opened to a cold audience. Nevertheless, there were some good
performances. Neville's bravura and mock-mad scene as Valentine

were highly praised, his use of his eyes in the latter being noted (Gielgud had played the part some years before at the Haymarket Theatre, and there were the inevitable comparisons owing to the actors' physical likeness: Neville, long incarcerated abroad in the Royal Navy and in the English provinces as an actor, had scarcely ever seen Gielgud and any acting similarities were and are entirely accidental and unconscious). Montague made 'a delightfully fresh and salty sailor', and Bird 'a lively, gusty, bull-voiced Sir Sampson Legend'. The beautiful Maxine Audley was the Angelica, Andrée Melly the country girl Miss Prue, Cairncross Foresight, Reynolds Mrs. Frail, Cartland Scandal and Richard Burrell Tattle. Slade wrote the music, and Joyce Hammond designed the sets.

Charles Morgan's *The River Line* on February 24th brought a distinguished contemporary and moving play by a dramatist whose quality has always made up for his limited quantity. It is a play of a tragic mistake in wartime France—the killing of a much-liked, spiritually serene young officer by his companions for suspected treachery when they are in hiding from the enemy—and its study is the effect of his vindication later on his killers. The theme is moral responsibility, the tragic miscalculations of destiny, and 'the peace that passeth all understanding'; but it is also an incisive play with a strong dramatic technique. At Bristol a young Canadian actor and producer, Donald Davis, played Philip Sturgess, Paul Scofield's part of the questioning American, and Bushell referred to Maureen Quinney's 'mystical radiance' as Valerie, the young girl (played by Virginia McKenna in town) on whose spirit at the last the spirit of the dead man, Heron, descends. The second act is the French one, and Heron's part not a long one: Neville, blond and *spirituelle*, was ideally cast. Maxine Audley was the French escape-organiser, Marie, and Robert Cartland her naval husband. The producer and company, according to the *Western Daily Press*, 'have trouble with the first act, achieve wonders of suspense with the second, and hold very well the climaxes of the last'.

The producer was Warren Jenkins, later to be responsible for several notable productions for the Bristol Old Vic, including the first performance in England of Arthur Miller's *The Crucible*. The 'cobwebs, shadows and junk' of the second-act disused French granary was designed by Patrick Robertson with immense feeling for atmosphere.

On March 17th came *The Duenna*, Julian Slade's second major work, later to be seen on television and in London, with several of the Bristol cast. Sheridan's only operetta had a run of seventy-five nights at Covent Garden in 1775—an unprecedented success for those days—and had been produced by Nigel Playfair at the Lyric, Hammersmith, in the 1920s; but it had not been seen in Bristol since near the end of the eighteenth century. Its libretto and lyrics are, in fact, expertly fashioned, and Byron thought it better than *The Beggar's Opera*, Hazlitt almost as good. Our own taste for the acid in satire would probably not endorse this, but *The Duenna* takes the stage with immense liveliness, and Slade's music, Sullivanesque in wit and variety of rhythm as well as tunefulness but without obvious *pastiche*, matched wit for wit and parody for parody. Alan Dent hailed the 'jolly and jaunty new score. . . . In his way—the old-fashioned, frankly melodious way of Offenbach and Sullivan which can never really go out of fashion—Mr. Slade is the gayest talent in light music since the deplorable loss of young Walter Leigh in the last war'.

A lightly gay production by Lionel Harris—never heavy-handed with the humour but rich in invention—helped the show to success (its three-week run was extended to four), and the company matched up with spirit. 'The great success of the evening', wrote the *Western Daily Press*, 'was Jane Wenham, much matured in personality since she was here four years ago and with a sweet soprano voice.' She is a witty singer as well as an actress as pretty and witty as King Charles's fabulous Nelly (a part she could surely enchantingly play?), and radiated later as Donna Luisa on television and at the Westminster Theatre. Gerald Cross gave a clever comedy performance as the Jewish suitor, Isaac Mendoza, which he also repeated in town, as David Bird repeated his irascible father, Don Jerome. Dorothy Reynolds was the comic Duenna (the *Western Daily Press* referred to her 'rich resource of foolery'), Maureen Quinney Donna Clara, and John Neville (with 'confident baritone') and James Cairncross were the two lovers. Elizabeth West and Richard Burrell danced and mimed Columbine and Harlequin, and Pat Robertson designed the settings and costumes (in London there were new designs by Tom Lingwood).

Ibsen's *The Wild Duck* on April 14th brought perhaps Neville's finest character performance while with the Bristol Old Vic Company, and his Gregers Werle was matched with Robert Eddison's Hjalmar Ekdal, Maureen Quinney's Hedwig (wringing

ABOVE: *Antony and Cleopatra*, 1953. Yvonne Coulette as Cleopatra with Carol Marsh (left) as Iras and Jeannette Sterke as Charmian.

BELOW: *Murder in the Cathedral* (T. S. Eliot), 1954. Eric Porter (left) as Becket and Basil Henson as the Fourth Tempter.

ABOVE: *Marching Song* (John Whiting), 1954. Edgar Wreford (right) as General Forster and Ronald Hines as Captain Bruno Hurst.

BELOW: *The Merchant of Venice*, 1955. Edgar Wreford (right) as Shylock and Michael Allinson as Antonio.

No Sign of the Dove (Peter Ustinov), 1954. Paul Lee as Matthew and
Perlita Neilson as Hope.

ABOVE: *The Two Bouquets* (Eleanor and Herbert Farjeon), 1954. L. *to* R. Catherine Hutchinson (Kate Gill), Edgar Wreford (Edward Gill), Paul Lee (Mr. Gill) and Phyllida Law (Laura Rivers).

BELOW: *Salad Days* (Reynolds–Slade), 1954. L. *to* R. John Warner (Timothy), Eric Porter (Uncle Zed), Norman Rossington (Electrode), Eleanor Drew (Jane) and Bob Harris (Troppo).

Both photos by Desmond Tripp

'every touch of happiness and every dreg of wretchedness from the part'), Dorothy Reynolds's Gina and Robert Cartland's Old Ekdal. 'The most exciting serious work by the Bristol Old Vic Company for many seasons', wrote the *Evening Post*: 'Its quality never wavers and there are no weaknesses.' There was, added the *Western Daily Press*, 'nothing heavy-handed about Denis Carey's production. In all its intense tragedy and comedy it has a liveliness'. 'If the Bristol Old Vic's production of *The Wild Duck* doesn't dispel the Ibsen Complex in Bristol, it is doubtful whether anything else will succeed in doing so', declared Bushell, who noted the 'impressive work by John Neville as Gregers—he moves with a bird-like agitation'. Eddison also won high praise: 'Mr. Eddison', wrote the *Manchester Guardian*, 'was particularly successful in suggesting the fluent schoolboy charm which had enslaved the young Gregers, even while the flawed glance and the weak rages, like the lashing of shallow water, betrayed the hollowness of the man. . . . On John Neville's Gregers Werle there were no reservations: here, terrifyingly, was the very type of purblind zealot. . . . Dorothy Reynolds gives Gina the huge calm of a June meadow.' Charles Radclyffe referred to Neville's 'quiet iciness'— 'a warped intellectual Nazi born fifty years before his time'—and conjured an apt picture of Eddison's Ekdal: 'Visually, he resembled Dante Gabriel Rossetti at a revivalist meeting, vocally, any great actor who is out of work and spends his time practising Cyrano.'

The great play, once again in Bristol history, made way for a frivolity. Anouilh's *Thieves' Carnival* proved one of the lighter *pièces roses*, which Carey's production precariously rescued. It was, wrote Bushell, 'mainly a triumph for the scenic designer. Hutchinson-Scott's exquisite good taste, which finds expression in the subtle blending of rich and delicate colour and his shrewd eye for form, has never served him better. . . . Denis Carey skilfully tries to gild this French trifle, and the result is something gay without being witty and lively without being more than mildly amusing'. He referred to Dorothy Reynolds 'sailing with a fixed resignation through a sea of ennui', and the general verdict on this 'charade with music', this very pale ring round a new and attenuated moon, was much the same. Most of the company were involved except Neville (soon to play Henry V). Slade composed, with dances by Yoma Sassburgh.

Henry V anticipated the Coronation by a few days on June 2nd, 1953; the last play of the season, it ran until June 20th and then transferred to the London Old Vic, where it was quickly and unfortunately overshadowed by the Birmingham Repertory Company's now historically famous production of the three parts of *Henry VI*, played in instalments on successive evenings. It was interesting to see how a Shakespearian play renowned for its popularity could not stand up to the unexpected juxtaposition of one (or, rather, three) equally renowned for their supposed 'unstageability', but it was not entirely a matter of interest in the less hackneyed. The *Henry VI*'s, or at any rate the second and third play, proved dramatically exciting, seething with character and conflict, superbly staged (by Douglas Seale) and magnificently spoken and acted: a combination the Bristol Old Vic production of *Henry V* could not emulate or suggest. Perhaps it was not the ideal play for this particular company, and certainly Denis Carey's economic mounting (two centre platforms, with curved steps leading to the corners of the set, a cyclorama and black curtains) could not take fire like Birmingham's equally economic but mobile and vivid heraldry. Again, too, Bristol tended to lack 'voices' (in which the Birmingham Company was rich) and the Old Vic stage in London did not so easily accommodate groupings and effects designed for the smaller, more intimate Bristol Theatre Royal.

Yet even in Bristol the play did not make a full effect, and Bushell's headline ran: 'Commons Outshine Royalty at Old Vic'. 'It is upon our imaginations that we must work, though the Chorus of Patrick McGoohan, who exhorts us to do this, is unleashed upon us with an astonishing savagery. Instead of gently coaxing these imaginary forces, Mr. McGoohan would bludgeon us into submission as he bludgeons the rich, sinewy verse at his disposal. . . . Neville moves with a stark dignity . . . but for all his zest and thrust he does not dominate the play.'

The truth is Neville needed a firmer production and greater 'weight' and experience. He was a Henry of brain, shrewdly appraising every diplomatic move, registering every bubble of suppressed anger, in the first scene, speaking eloquently throughout, and deeply sincere, particularly in the scene of the slaying of the luggage boys. But although A. E. Wilson praised his 'fire and impetuosity' it was not the general view: he lacked the dynamism of the truly dominating Henry. Kenneth Tynan recognised in the performance a budding Richard II—a shrewd stroke, for Henry's cunning in the first scenes is not unlike Richard's, and Neville later was to give a brilliant characterisation of Richard II at the London Old Vic. Nevertheless, his Henry, not yet quite ripe, showed abundant intelligence and natural talent, which many remembered when he moved, a few weeks later, into the 1953-4 London Old Vic Company.

The London critics were lukewarm on the production—Ivor Brown's 'moderate efficiency' descending to Tynan's 'solidly second-rate'—but Harold Hobson glowed rightly about Dorothy Reynolds's moving description of Falstaff's end. James Cairncross played Pistol, Richard Burrell Nym, McGoohan MacMorris, David Bird a rather heavy and too-juicy Fluellen, Robert Cartland Constable of France, Lee Montague Lewis the Dauphin, Gerald Cross Charles VI, Yvonne Coulette Alice and Maureen Quinney Katherine. Peter Bryant was a delightful Cockney Boy, the performance that strangely most lingers across the years. Patrick Robertson designed.

In June the company also flew to Zürich, where *Henry V* had a more gratifying response. It was not to be the last successful appearance of the Bristol Old Vic Company at the Zürich Festival.

[A.W.]

CHAPTER TEN

The Ninth Season
1953 *to* 1954

IN SEPTEMBER 1953, at the beginning of the ninth season, Denis Carey had been at Bristol for three years. His tenure of office now equalled that which had been enjoyed by Hugh Hunt. There was no definite term of contract but Carey himself believed that no director should stay too long in this onerous position. This point of view was not shared by Alfred Francis, the administrator of the Old Vic, who pointed out to Carey that William Armstrong, whose work in the North had wielded so important an influence on the British Theatre as a whole, had been for twenty-two years the director of the Liverpool Playhouse. If Carey were to put the Mecca of London out of his mind, there was no reason why he should not, if he so wished, settle down for life at Bristol. No one would be better pleased than the Bristolians. Eventually Carey agreed to stay at least one more year, stating that he would give his decision as to the future in the spring of 1954.

In the preceding two years Carey had had frequent absences from Bristol, producing at the Old Vic in London and at Stratford-on-Avon. Sometimes these productions had not dovetailed, and they had tended to disorganise the Bristol programme. A postponed production of *Twelfth Night* in the Waterloo Road did, in fact, unsettle the 1953 autumn season in Bristol, producing a programme which was of not too good a shape, and consequently had sparse financial results. At the turn of the year, although the decision was not announced until March of 1954, Denis determined that the season was to be his last at Bristol, and that, moreover, he would give it his undivided attention—accept no outside engagements, and do everything to ensure a brilliant climax to his work. Thanks to *Salad Days* he succeeded beyond his wildest expectations.

Salad Days now belongs to history, and there is little left that can be said about it. One hitherto unrecorded incident is, however, worth relating. During the first fortnight of its run at Bristol, in spite of the paeans of praise in the Bristol Press, and the packed houses, so unusual in summertime, I could persuade no London manager to interest himself in the venture. It was not until the Tuesday of the last week that the first London agent arrived, and from that moment forward the news spread like wildfire through the Shaftesbury Avenue and Piccadilly offices. I was due to go down to Bristol on the Friday, but on the Thursday Denis phoned me and asked me to come down immediately. I arrived that evening to find the Theatre Royal invaded by the most important people from the West End Theatre. After the show there was one well-known manager sitting in Denis Carey's office, whilst I interviewed Jack Hylton and Jack Gatti in Tom Hickson's office. Outside in the bar, Bill Linnit fretted and fumed. Eventually it was these three, as a result of negotiations concluded by Alfred Francis, who were to be jointly responsible for putting on the show in London. Rarely, however, in any theatre can a manager have been confronted with such competition for the purchase of his wares.

Carey's period of office had come to an end. In July 1954 he was given a luncheon in Bristol, with Sir Philip Morris in the chair. There were present members of the Bristol Corporation, Alderman Chamberlain and Alderman Watson Allan; other prominent citizens, such as Robert Lyne and his wife, Veronica, and several of the Governors of the Old Vic, including Mrs. Patricia Strauss, Hamish Hamilton and Lady Violet Bonham-Carter. The latter made a brilliant speech, full of the biting wit for which she is so justly famous. Proposing the toast to Britain's oldest living theatre, she apologised for the cheek of the 'upstarts' at the London Old Vic, who had rechristened their illustrious forbear in Bristol after themselves, 'Compared with you, we are only in our "Salad Days" ', she said, and went on: 'History records that long before the battle of Waterloo or the battle of Waterloo Road were won, the Theatre Royal was in the field victorious. Let's salute it in gratitude.'

Carey departed to London, to enter the hazardous whirlpool of free-lance work. *Salad Days* safeguarded his immediate financial future, and enabled him to pick and choose his productions. It was not long before he added the brilliance of *Romanoff and Juliet* to his wreath of laurels.   [C.L.]

It was the Irish in Carey which probably responded to *The Castiglioni Brothers*. He had seen this farcical comedy by Alberto

Colantuoni in Italy three years before, and the *Western Daily Press* headline the day after the first night (September 7th, 1953)— 'Curtain Up on Chaos'—gives a clue to its appeal to a producer always at his best in a gregarious romp. The plot concerned a missing winning lottery ticket and the frantic search for it by the family of the deceased winner. 'Denis Carey's fourth season as director of the Bristol Old Vic began last night with the "Harry Lime Theme" ', wrote the *Western Daily Press*. '. . . the first impression is one of stunned astonishment that anyone could possibly live in such disorder. Nothing seems to be in place except the needle on the gramophone.' The family are, in fact, searching for the lottery ticket, which still evades detection after the house seems literally to have been pulled to pieces. It was obviously 'a producer's play', and although it would, as a critic pointed out, be little without inventive direction and contained scarcely a witty line, its fun waxed to the end.

'A season could hardly start with a company pulling more fantastic faces, and when those faces are wed to David Bird's raspberry roar and sizzling intakes of breath, one could laugh all night whatever the play', wrote the *Western Daily Press* again. Patrick Robertson's set was described as 'a masterpiece of designed untidiness' and the cast included many from previous seasons: Patrick McGoohan, Dorothy Reynolds, Yvonne Coulette, Lee Montague, Carol Marsh, Robert Cartland (as a lawyer gradually intoxicated), Norman Rossington and John Warner. Newcomers were James Maxwell and Alan Dobie, further recuits who had been trained in the Old Vic Dramatic School: both were to play later at the London Old Vic, and Dobie was to return to Bristol in 1955 and 1956 to play leading parts with distinction. Pat Heywood, later of *Salad Days*, was also new, and Phyllida Law returned after a season in small parts at the London Vic.

The Cherry Orchard on September 29th was produced by John Moody, who was to be Carey's successor as director of the company the following season. He aimed at comedy, and printed extracts in the programme from Tchehov's own letters complaining that the Moscow Arts Theatre production made his characters 'cry-babies' and distorted the whole play, which was 'a comedy, in places almost a farce'. He also restored some passages in Act II which were cut by Stanislavsky in production, and were translated by David Magarshack in his book *Chekhov the Dramatist*.

This was, of course, all very impressive, and two Bristol critics were duly impressed by the result: Peter Rodford, now critic of the *Western Daily Press*, saw 'a gentle, sympathetic wedding of laughter and tears', and Dennis Bushell thought 'Mr. Moody and his cast work with such skill that they almost persuade us into thinking they have discovered a new play, so different is their *Cherry Orchard* from others'.

Only John Coe was flatly dubious: 'the play calls for the finest playing and it is my quarrel with last night's performance that that is just what it did not receive'. I saw the play on the last night, when it certainly had had time to 'play itself in', and I ally myself absolutely with Coe. It is, of course, exaggerated to suggest other modern English productions of *The Cherry Orchard* have missed the comedy: one has only to remember Tyrone Guthrie's for the Old Vic at the New Theatre in 1941. Sad and merry (and it is, of course, both) it is a warm, shimmering, utterly human play, and my main memory of Moody's *The Cherry Orchard* is of a strange bleakness. Partly this was due to Robertson's settings, predominantly blue-green and cold, with a chilly nursery and those cut-off tops characteristic of the expressionistic stage. The certainty of feeling remains that Tchehov needs realism—they are plays of life, without (except in *The Seagull*) the conscious symbols that make such production sometimes possible with Ibsen. And their poetry, too, springs a great deal from surrounding Nature: the forests that fascinate Astrov in *Uncle Vanya*, the moonlit lake of *The Seagull*, the doomed cherry orchard, signature of a dying past, in this play. Here the shadow of a white blossom never fell, and the imagination of Dorothy Reynolds's Madame Ranevsky, unaided by set or atmosphere, proved not strong enough to conjure it.

Although sincere and capable of weeping real tears, this fine actress, with her gaunt bone-structure and strength rather than luminosity of personality, was in fact miscast as Tchehov's resilient, feckless, warm and iridescent heroine. Yvonne Coulette, dark and irritably smouldering, was happier as Varya, and a guest player, John Arnatt, who had been the handsome and impressive Richard, Duke of York, in the Birmingham Repertory *Henry VI*'s, gave a most distinguished performance as Léonid Gaev, with a wry irony and indolent delicacy of touch that were wholly Tchehovian in style (he had received high praise also for his Dr.

Dorn in *The Seagull* at the Arts Theatre some time before). This was the only performance of real charm, except perhaps for John Warner's wistfully clumsy and unlucky Yepikhodof. Carol Marsh was a pretty Anya, Alan Dobie, still not quite perfect in senile make-up, a promising Feers, David Bird a rather heavy-handed Lopákhin, Pat Heywood Dunyasha, Lee Montague Yasha, and Robert Cartland Pishtchick. But none of them were really memorable or seemed to get, collectively, the 'feel' of the play.

Antony and Cleopatra, that most difficult exercise in large-scale tragedy, was the next bold choice, and surprisingly achieved more than partial success on the tiny stage. 'Denis Carey and the Bristol Old Vic', wrote Bushell, 'have given us their best Shakespeare since they rediscovered *The Two Gentlemen of Verona*. The picture that emerges is vivid and compelling, even if the characters do not assume the major proportions of Shakespeare and convey passion on the grand scale. . . . Yvonne Coulette's Cleopatra suggests more of the kitten than the Serpent of Old Nile in the first half of the play . . . but the character suddenly grows in stature, finally to achieve queenly dignity and pathos.'

John Coe, too, thought the slenderly beautiful Yvonne Coulette won her battle against a tremendous part: 'Now the first things one looks for in Cleopatra are voluptuousness and ruthlessness. But nature has not ordained that Miss Coulette should either look voluptuous or suggest ruthlessness. If this tremendous character was to engulf Antony it had to be based on the actress's technical resources; it had to overcome her physical limitations. Miss Coulette's resources won the fight. This is certainly not the ideal Cleopatra, but in its own way it is a remarkable creation.'

Douglas Campbell returned to play Antony, and he had by nature the physique and stature for the part, if not the full emotional passion and moving qualities of the mature tragic heroic actor: 'As Antony', wrote Coe, 'Douglas Campbell, burly and handsome, met the physical challenge of the part unflinchingly. He also met the intellectual demands fairly and squarely. Here was a man ravaged by dissoluteness and vanity—a great general gone to seed.' Montague's Enobarbus he described as 'a graphic reporter and a moving figure of loyalty abused', and Bushell commented on John Warner's 'shrewd and coldly calculating Octavius'. Carol Marsh and Jeanette Sterke (who had been a darkly pretty Anne Bullen in the London Old Vic's Coronation production of *Henry*

VIII, her first professional performance) were Iras and Charmian, Dobie (whose set little face thrives on the mystically remote) was the Soothsayer, McGoohan Pompey, Cartland Agrippa, Daniel Thorndike Lepidus and Reynolds (rather strangely) Octavia. Robertson's sets were simple and practical, of necessity, but beautiful and variegated by lighting. The play was, wrote the *Western Daily Press*, 'directed with a firmness and forthrightness that brings immense force to what is indeed a great work'.

Old Bailey, a new play on November 10th, 1953, attracted a good deal of attention as the first play of a leading dramatic critic, T. C. Worsley of the *New Statesman and Nation*. It was greeted with respect rather than enthusiasm. A play representing the conflict between the older and younger generations, with a rather Galsworthian *Old English* background of a family 'in trade', it was preceded by a 'Narration' between two characters in the present time, the main play being a flashback to 1923.

Patrick Gibbs of the *Daily Telegraph* thought 'the conflict would have been more effective had the adversaries been more positive in character' and lack of deep and dramatically exciting character interest was generally felt to be a weakness of the play. The dominating character of Robert Bailey—'Old Bailey'—tenaciously holding on to the business architecture of his own building, was played by Douglas Campbell, who won high praise. The young actor Richard Johnson appeared for the first time with the company as Jack Bailey, with Sheila Sweet, another newcomer and later of the TV Family Grove, as his wife. The 'regulars' played the other parts, under Peter Potter (of the Arts Council and Salisbury Playhouse, where Carey had been) as producer.

Sean O'Casey's *The End of the Beginning* and Shakespeare's *The Comedy of Errors*, on December 1st, provided a light 'double bill'. Nat Brenner produced the first, which with David Bird, Norman Rossington and Dorothy Reynolds in the three parts aroused much mirth. *The Comedy* was very much up Carey's street, and the production, wrote Coe, was 'stamped with the authority of the man who understands the technique of farce'. 'The triumph of controlled chaos in the Irish kitchen', complemented Rodford, 'was equalled by the achievement of organised disorder in the streets of Ephesus.' (The streets were the work of Rosemary Vercoe, whose designs reminded one critic of the Pied Piper's Hamelin.) Alan Dobie and John Warner, whose small, pointed faces are in fact not dissimilar, were the Dromio twins: 'impish, impertinent and imperishable', in Rodford's happy alliteration. Richard Johnson and a newcomer from filmland, Russel Enoch, were the elegant Antipholus twins, Daniel Thorndike Aegeon, Cartland the Duke of Ephesus, and Reynolds, Coulette and Sheila Shand-Gibbs the three women, Emelia, Adriana and Luciana.

The Christmas show, *The Merry Gentleman*, was another success by Dorothy Reynolds and Julian Slade, involving three Father Christmasses (one authentic, two impostors) and an episode 'In Christmasland' in which James Cairncross distinguished himself as a Snowman ('melting gently through the door', an intriguing feat, at the end of his song) and also (like Warner, Dobie and Bob Harris) transformed himself into a reindeer. In domesticated mood he also managed to be a paterfamilias. David Bird was Father Christmas, Dorothy Reynolds one 'Aunt Mabel', Norman Rossington gave a 'wickedly witty study of a modern photographer at work', and John Warner (when un-horned) shone as a young man struck by shyness when without his umbrella. Jane Wenham again returned to sing her way back into Bristol hearts, and was joined by Joan Plowright, inevitably from the Old Vic Dramatic School, who 'with an affecting catch in her voice' made 'a most disarming lovelorn maiden'. The two were to be paired again in the London production of *The Duenna*, before Joan Plowright made her outstanding success as Wycherley's Country Wife, and attracted attention in other parts, at the Royal Court Theatre. The production was by Lionel Harris (of *The Duenna*), with settings and costumes by Tom Lingwood and dances by Elizabeth West.

Clifford Odets's *Winter Journey*, on February 23rd, 1954, brought Eric Porter to the Bristol Old Vic, to play the complex part of the drunken actor, Frank Elgin, created by Michael Redgrave in town. It is a part which seems destined to be associated with Old Vic players. Both Redgrave and his London successor, Alexander Knox, have done distinguished work at the Old Vic (Knox before the war achieved his first success there and was the Cardinal Wolsey of the Coronation *Henry VIII*), and at the Birmingham Repertory the part was played by Edgar Wreford, who also migrated to the Vic and became Bristol's leading man in the 1954-5 season.

Porter, like Wreford, was a young Birmingham Repertory

actor who had distinguished himself there while still in his mid-twenties in a series of character parts of all ages, and had in 1953 played Bolingbroke in *Richard II* and other parts in John Gielgud's season at the Lyric, Hammersmith. Elgin is a character with a mental 'twist'—his psychological interest being less in the addiction to drink that has ruined his career, and threatens his 'come-back', than in a strange complexity of nature, an inferiority complex undermining his actor's vanity, which causes him subtly, and almost to his own as well as other people's deception, to suggest that his downfall springs from flaws in the character of his loyal and devoted wife. He is an absorbing character to play for this reason, requiring both emotional power in a climax and an altogether subtler intellectual detachment in the psychological portrait (Redgrave and Wreford, both actors deeply interested in the Stanislavsky theories of acting, must have found him a subject which fascinatingly responded to their intellectual and emotional approach). Porter made the expected success, being 'completely convincing as the actor gone to seed', in Coe's estimate, and finding compassion as well as self-pity in the portrait. He is an actor attuned to the neurotic part, and more at home on the stage in middle age than his own youth.

Yvonne Coulette played the wife ('the best work she has done for the company', wrote Coe) and Basil Henson the major part of the producer in which Sam Wanamaker had first exploded on London. The play's fault is its not wholly convincing happy ending—characters with a twist, like Elgin, are not so easily unravelled even by success—but it won Bristol's respect in Denis Carey's production.

To Dekker's *Shoemaker's Holiday*, on March 16th, Carey took like a duck to water. 'There is no such mirror of contemporary Elizabethan and Jacobean life as is offered us in the works of Dekker, no author who has given us more of the London life of the time', proclaimed a programme note, and Carey plunged with Irish flamboyance into the seething City life of sixteenth-century London, and a plethora of characters surrounding Simon Eyre, the master shoemaker, who was actually founded on an historic figure, a draper who came to London and found fame and fortune among the tradesmen.

Douglas Campbell played Simon and John Warner Fisk, his journeyman. 'Both are priceless assets to the Old Vic', was a critical comment. Dorothy Reynolds was Margery, Simon's wife, Alan Dobie and Yvonne Coulette Ralph, the other journeyman, and Jane, his wife, Eric Porter and Geoffrey Taylor two City merchants, Basil Henson the Earl of Lincoln, Michael Meacham the hero-lover Lacey ('admirably combining the talents of clown, musician and juvenile lead') and Christine Finn (who had been Barrie's Boy David at the Birmingham Repertory and Ophelia and Olivia in *Twelfth Night* in Laurence Payne's Shakespeare season at the Embassy Theatre) Simon's pretty daughter Rose. Taylor, a newcomer prominent later at the Birmingham Repertory Theatre, also played 'a decorative, commanding and human Henry VIII.'

The School for Wives (Molière's *L'Ecole des Femmes*) brought back the ever-welcome Miles Malleson in a record-breaking success. Produced at the Palais Royal on December 26th, 1662, Molière's classic story is of the jealous elderly Arnolphe who adopts a child of six years old in order to train her to be the ideal docile wife, only to find himself duped by the 'innocent' when she has attained the necessary and most seductive age. Malleson ('who flops and gasps and bulges like the frog that would a-wooing go', wrote *The Times*) was as Arnolphe scarcely ever off the stage, and *The Times* conceded that he justified 'in his own performance many of the liberties he takes with his author'. Eric Porter's 'superbly cynical' Chrysalde, and the 'innocence and ardour' of Christine Finn and Michael Meacham as the adopted Agnes and her lover, were commented on, and there was expert support from Warner, Dobie, Basil Henson and Pat Heywood. Denis Carey produced with designs by Patrick Robertson, who created a mobile form of setting which could be changed in full view of the audience.

T. S. Eliot's *Murder in the Cathedral* on May 11th, 1954, was a triumph for Eric Porter and brought Bristol Old Vic audiences the opportunity to see a third play by the poet. The play had been revived the previous year by Robert Helpmann at the London Old Vic, in a production which gave new dramatic force to the tragedy (with a brilliant comedy interlude with the satiric apologetic knights), and was distinguished by a memorable performance of Becket by Robert Donat, incomparable in eloquence and spiritual integrity. Carey's Bristol production, with settings by Robertson of 'simple dignity and grandeur', also created a considerable impression on many. John Bennett found the performance 'something richly and vividly exciting and majestically wonderful', with perfect lighting by Nat Brenner and a 'deeply sincere and compelling performance by Eric Porter' (as Becket). 'It is more than faultless: it is an inspired piece of acting without a false moment in it. . . . Of Mr. Carey's productions that I have seen, this is easily the finest.' Coe commented on the nobility of Porter's portrait, and only Rodford (headline: 'Full Impact not Achieved') was not completely impressed. 'As Becket, Eric Porter gives a performance of physical and mental force, but not of mental uplift. He is at his most gripping when he is wrestling with the temptations of the past or defying the threats of his murderers, but in his Christmas morning sermon, quietly, smoothly spoken without excessive gesture, there seems little warmth of human feeling and little, either, to link it with the divine.' Among professionals, Miles Malleson and his wife, the television producer Tania Lieven, were enormously impressed by Porter's performance, which they thought put him in the potential class of a star actor; and both have the eye of the practising producer as well as the actor. Certainly, the echoes of Porter's success reached the Old Vic and other theatre circles in London, and he was to migrate to the parent Old Vic company in the coming autumn season.

Alan Dobie, the First Priest of Helpmann's London Old Vic production, at Bristol played Third Priest with his compelling last speech; George Selway was First Knight (Paul Rogers's success at the London Old Vic); and John Warner, who had played First Tempter in London ('Fluting in the meadows, viols in the hall, Laughter and apple-blossom floating on the water'), repeated this performance with the addition of Third Knight at Bristol. Yvonne Coulette had led the Women of Canterbury in London; she did so again, with Dorothy Reynolds, Christine Finn, Eleanor Drew and Pat Heywood in a compact team.

On June 1st, without a hint of prophecy, *Salad Days*, the Reynolds-Slade 'summer' musical, burst sunnily upon an unsuspecting Bristol. The happy enchantment of this artless but amusing 'comedy with music', an expert blending of the revue sketch with a gay little story of Minnie, the magic piano, who makes all hearers throw away their cares and dance, is now a matter of London as well as Bristol theatre history. Carved to the versatile acting talents of the resident company, it lost nothing by a few changes of cast when, with ex-Bristol Old Vic substitutes for Alan Dobie (the Bristol Tramp), Eric Porter (Uncle Clam,

Manager of the Cleopatra Night Club, Ambrose and Uncle Zed) and Norman Rossington (P.C. Boot and Electrode), it was whisked to town to embark on an apparently perennial non-stop run at the Vaudeville Theatre. Its Bristol teamwork was still assured with Newton Blick, Michael Aldridge and James Cairncross sharing the leading parts acted by Dobie and Porter, and with John Warner and the charming singer Eleanor Drew still playing the young lovers, Timothy and Jane. Dorothy Reynolds's series of portraits, from taciturn beautician to *couturier's* model and blonde nightclub singer (sand in her eyes), were in both towns a satiric tower of strength, and in both towns too Julian Slade himself continued to play one of the two pianos which form the musical accompaniment.

Julian Slade had intended the part of Jane for Jane Wenham, who could not play it at the time but did so later on a tour of Germany and for a fortnight at the Vaudeville Theatre when the regular company went on holiday. Here again a number of the cast were ex-Bristol Old Vic or Shakespearian players (James Maxwell and David Dodimead shared some Aldridge parts), and later in the first Canadian production Mary Savidge (Bristol Old Vic leading lady of the 1954-5 season), who happened to be in Canada for a broadcasting engagement, found herself swept by an almost inevitable destiny into the Dorothy Reynolds roles.

Salad Days, with its timeless and haunting Julian Slade tunes and unshadowed sense of fun, has not merely taken a leading part in a revival of the British musical, but acts as an ambassador for the Bristol Old Vic wherever it is played. It is charming now to read John Bennett's cautious prophecy on June 2nd, 1954: 'It's due to run for three weeks; I think they could pack the theatre for twice that time to see this happy production.'

Graham Greene's *The Living Room*, Carey's last production as Director of the Bristol Old Vic, was a sombrely uncharacteristic choice which played from June 22nd to July 10th, 1954.

Harold Hobson wrote the programme note, describing the play as 'full of paradoxes'.

> For example, it is a religious play, and it sounds irreligious; it is a play by a Roman Catholic, and it sounds anti-Catholic; it is a play about a man, and nearly everyone takes it to be a play about a woman.

The young girl's part in it undoubtedly is magnificent, and it made Dorothy Tutin, who played it in London, the most sought-after actress in the West End. But in my opinion the central character is the priest, the man who waits for twenty years for the opportunity to prove his usefulness, and then, when the opportunity comes, thinks that he has missed it. . . .

The *Living Room* is the best first play of the last thirty years; and it is one of the finest plays in any category.

Certainly it is a tragedy to stick in the mind, poignant in its failure—which is humanity's failure—to solve the dilemmas of moral responsibility and the conflict of the flesh and the devil. They have been exercising dramatists since medieval times, and if Greene descends to a certain cheapening with his emphasis on physical details and false prudery (the house of the sisters Browne is a terrifying and depressing one), he does present the dilemmas with a real passionate conviction of their urgency to the people involved.

Christine Finn had the testing part of Rose, the girl driven by the conflict to suicide: she was, wrote John Coe, 'splendid in the second act when her torment reaches breaking point, but less effective in the first'. Eric Porter played Eric Portman's part of the crippled Priest impressively in the final stage of the tragedy, and Jane Eccles (the gentle one) and Dorothy Reynolds (the fierce uncharitable one) were the aunts, Teresa and Helen Browne. Basil Henson as Rose's distressed lover and Yvonne Coulette as his unhappy, neurotic wife completed the small cast. Robertson designed.

Carey's valediction was a tribute to Bristol and the theatre its citizens had preserved. After eight years the Bristol Old Vic 'is no longer', he declared, 'an experiment. It is an institution. It has become part of the city's heritage. . . . The Bristol Old Vic is now the leading repertory theatre in the country. . . .'

This was and is so nearly the exact truth that one feels inclined to leave Sir Barry Jackson and the Birmingham Repertory Theatre to meet the challenge in their own way: through their productions and the splendid players they have actually often passed on to, or in their turn received from, the Bristol Old Vic. [A.W.]

CHAPTER ELEVEN

The Tenth Season
1954 *to* 1955

JOHN MOODY, who was now in charge at Bristol, had up to the time of his appointment been for five years the drama director of the Arts Council, and as such his connection with Bristol had been intimate. He was, in fact, making a return to the Old Vic. He had started as an actor with the organisation in London in the 1930s, and at the outbreak of the war was in charge of the school attached to the Waterloo Road. Later he became the director of the Old Vic Company which, during the war, flourished at the Liverpool Playhouse, and subsequently he was producer of opera for the sister organisation of Sadler's Wells. As a member of the management committee of the Bristol Old Vic he was, of course, well aware of all its problems.

One of the most pressing problems at the time of his appointment was that of the school, and here his knowledge and his administrative experience were eagerly sought. The school had been Hugh Hunt's 'baby', but Denis Carey, one-minded as a producer, had frankly never taken a very great interest in it. Sir Philip Morris, to whom the school had always been of great concern, had set up a sub-committee late in 1953 to inquire into its past and future. This sub-committee, under the chairmanship of Alfred Francis, and with John Moody as a member, had reported that unless better premises could be found, and unless more money could be made available for the payment of a more experienced staff, the school really had no future. For a time no action was taken, but in May 1954, a month before Carey was due to leave, Edward Stanley resigned. He had been in charge of the school for eight years, and during that time had managed to keep it in being under abnormal difficulties.

One of the terms of Moody's contract was, therefore, that in addition to being director of the company, he should also assume full responsibility for the school. His first task would be to suggest a new head, whose title would be 'Principal' whilst

Moody was titled Director of the School. He chose Duncan Ross, who had been with the Young Vic Company, and was at the time manager at the Nottingham Playhouse. He was a young man in his early thirties, and the appointment was, without question, an admirable one. New blood and young new ideas were introduced.

Little progress, however, could be made without the new premises, but, luckily, the picture had now changed, thanks to the golden profits of *Salad Days*. Money was available and buildings were no longer so scarce in Bristol. Once more the personality of Tom Hickson was brought into play. He found a block of two Victorian houses in Clifton, and before any rival could move he secured an option on behalf of the school. The purchase and furnishing required more money than was, at that time, available from *Salad Days*, so other quarters were approached, and thanks to Sir Philip Morris a handsome grant came from the Dulverton Trust, followed by an additional grant from the Old Vic Trust. For the next twelve months the whole time was taken up equipping the school in such a manner that, when it was officially opened in the summer of 1956, Sir Philip Morris could justly and proudly claim that it was the best-equipped drama school in the country.

As a director of the company, Moody took one determined move. At the Arts Council he had been greatly concerned in the schemes for nurturing new playwrights, and he was convinced that the function of a company like the Bristol Old Vic, if it was to claim national status, must be to lay a greater emphasis than hitherto on the modern play. His selection of Arthur Miller's play, *The Crucible* for production early in his first season at once brought a focus on the company. Surprise was expressed by the London Press that 'so important a play by a writer of international status should be performed for the first time in this country by a repertory—even though it be a leading repertory like the Bristol Old Vic Company'. Gradually, however, and especially after the production of *The Mulberry Bush* and *Ondine* in Moody's second season, it began to be taken for granted that a première at Bristol might be as important as one in Shaftesbury Avenue. That has been John Moody's great achievement at Bristol.   [C.L.]

That John Moody's policy was to be one in which contemporary plays of intellectual quality took a large part was apparent from the inclusion of John Whiting's controversial *Marching Song* and Arthur Miller's *The Crucible* (which had never been performed in England) in his programme for the first half of the season (Shaw's *The Devil's Disciple*, originally planned as part of the repertoire, was also replaced later by Peter Ustinov's *No Sign of the Dove*, which like *Marching Song* had had a very short run in town and aroused conflict of opinion). Moody felt, rightly, that it was in theatres such as the Bristol Old Vic that a ready-made serious audience might be found for such plays, and artistic managements of this kind had an obligation to take some financial risks which the short runs of the repertoire system made possible. His boldness of choice was not always to be financially successful, but the artistic results often gave prestige to the theatre.

Nevertheless, he chose to open on August 30th, 1954, with a now rarely played eighteenth-century comedy, Thomas Holcroft's *The Road to Ruin*, which had fallen into disuse though once popular with leading actors (Fay Compton, acting at the London Old Vic with Edgar Wreford at the time the play was decided on, immediately remembered it as an excellent comedy in which her father often played). First produced at Covent Garden in 1792, it is typical of the period (like *The School for Scandal*, a link between Restoration comedy and later romanticism), and though not equalling Sheridan in wit or literary style, it acts amusingly owing to a well-contrived comedy plot and many opportunities for characterisation. Its scapegrace hero, Harry Dornton, is, like Charles Surface, a disarming rogue, with a father who like Sir Oliver rails and threatens disinheritance while secretly loving the boy. An amorous widow, Mrs. Warren, with an eligible daughter is much in the Lady Wishford tradition; Mr. Silky, a Jewish moneylender, is of course a prototype of Moses (though a richer part), and the horsy Charles Goldfinch, involved with the widow, is a rather flashier Tony Lumpkin.

Moody had gathered together a good company, in which mature experience and youthful promise were better balanced than in some of his later seasons, and at least two of his players, Mary Savidge and Edgar Wreford, were to prove not only artists of high quality but quite outstandingly versatile. Mary Savidge had been a student at the Old Vic School when it was under Moody's direction before the war, and had attracted notice at the Oxford Repertory in many leading roles, including Jennet in *The Lady's*

Not for Burning, a poetic part to which her unusually beautiful and mellow voice had specially fitted her. As the raddled widow Warren her gifts of high comedy and character were pronounced, although the make-up by some standards was rather over-caricatured. Wreford was a thirty-year-old actor from the Birmingham Repertory (he had brilliantly 'doubled' Humphrey, Duke of Gloucester, and Richard 'Crookback' in their productions of *Henry VI*) and the London Old Vic, where the previous season he had shown his range as the Gravedigger and First Player in *Hamlet*, the virulent elderly tribune Sicinius in *Coriolanus*, and Hubert in *King John*. A serious, cultured actor and personality but with reserves of vital charm, he achieved an astonishing meta-morphosis of looks and temperament as the brash, cheerful, whipcracking and oafish Goldfinch: a transformation the Bristol audience obviously could not as yet fully relish. Like so many of our most talented and rising players, he was trained in the Old Vic Dramatic School under Michel St. Denis, Glen Byam Shaw and George Devine, and was in its first group of students at its opening after the war.

Michael Allinson, a little older than Wreford, played young Dornton with a period elegance (that elegance in which lace ruffles seem to *grow* from the wrists) and a charm that made one wish to see him as Charles Surface: he carried his impudences lightly, but just failed to convince in the famous 'drunk' scene. He was an experienced actor of good voice and presence, who had played with the Lunts in town and with [John Clements and Kay Hammond in *The Beaux' Stratagem*. John Kidd, a still more experienced player, well known for his fine character work at Stratford-on-Avon and the Old Vic, was the older Dornton, a City banker: it was not, perhaps, his best part, but his presence in the company (unfortunately only for a few months) was to provide valuable maturity and balance. Paul Lee, as Mr. Sulky his partner, endearingly suggested a heart of gold under a sullen exterior; again he was a thoroughly equipped player, who had also been producer for the Midland Theatre Company sponsored by the Arts Council. His exceptionally warm, gentle personality and beautiful voice were to prove great assets.

Bruce Sharman, though much younger, was like Wreford a product of the Old Vic Dramatic School and a member of last season's London Old Vic company; his portrait of the elderly

Jew was a brilliant piece of character comedy, widely praised. John Cairney as Harry's friend showed an arresting and attractive face and personality: a young, and technically still rather raw, Scots actor from the Glasgow Citizens' Theatre, who was to graduate to better parts later. The only performance which really misfired was Perlita Neilson's Sophia Truelove, the widow's daughter, which the producer allowed to be played far too archly for comfort in an unnatural high-pitched voice. This small actress had given a clever and emotionally moving performance as the child Marquise in Aimée Stuart's play, *Lace on her Petticoat*, in London and New York, and was only just graduating to older parts: she was to 'grow' impressively (metaphorically speaking) in the coming season, and soon afterwards achieve London success as Nina in *The Seagull* and in *The Diary of Anne Frank*. By that time she had also married her Bristol colleague, Bruce Sharman.

Unfortunately the settings were not particularly attractive and some mishaps in scene-shifting on the first night had a share in inspiring cooler notices than the acting itself deserved. The play gained pace and smoothness later, but it was never an outstanding production.

Moody's production of *Marching Song* was altogether more successful and in most ways better—warmer, deeper, and more intimately human—than the London one. He was helped in this by Patrick Robertson's fine set with its less chilling contemporary ring and vista of distant mountains, and a more central 'placing' of the ancient soldier's helmet which is so vital to the action and the character of General Forster. He was helped, too, by having in Edgar Wreford, in the enormously important and complex role of the disgraced General, an actor who was temperamentally and intellectually deeply responsive to character and play, and ready to probe well below the surface to Whiting's inner idea.

Wreford had seen the play with me at the St. Martin's Theatre a short while before the Bristol engagement was offered him, and it was then his second visit. 'I "knew" about Rupert when I first saw the play', he wrote during the Bristol production, and his portrayal, though different from the London one of Robert Flemyng (who had impressively suggested the General bitter, reticent, yet haunted in defeat, a man of action and ambition withering at the root), did illumine certain aspects of the character which seem inherent in the contemporary nature of the theme:

an inward resignation—the equivalent of sainthood perhaps in a religious man—and acceptance which Wreford himself described as 'a kind of "calm guilt" '. 'He doesn't *reject* anything—he has just moved forward to a new centre.'

Wreford was rather too young for the character (it was the only criticism made later by Whiting, who attended the last rehearsals) and the intended wig having proved unsuitable he was obliged to play the part throughout the run in hair which was too long and out of prison character (he was growing it for his next part, Benedick: contrasts in hair styles are among the bugbears of the actor and actress in repertory). But he had this striking sense of spiritual detachment ('calm guilt') and the power to project an altogether maturer mind and experience of life, and his performance was an impressive one which became moving (rightly through its restraint) in the two great speeches in which Rupert Forster recalls his killing of the child in war, impeded advance, and new understanding of humanity: the sense of 'blood on his sleeve'.

Marching Song is a play of a modern city in defeat, after the occupying army has left, but it centres its contemporary comment, which reaches out beyond the immediate to all human and moral responsibility, in its few selected characters: the General, scape-goat for defeat; the young girl, Dido, with her free, hard young modern philosophy picked up in the turbulent streets; the General's rich mistress, Catherine, too shallow now for his detached, bruised mind and awareness of spiritual dilemma, for all her poignant loyalty to a shattered past; the Prime Minister, John Cadmus, cynically facing the democratisation of a defeated totalitarian State; the unhappy, average-minded film producer whose triumphs were all of the 'silent' era; at the last, the young totalitarian Captain to whom the General with his new conscience is a fallen idol, and who will drive on ruthlessly through the same recurring dilemma of civilisation.

Yet the General never fully grasps at his moral responsibility: he is aware of it, but monastically, from outside the pull of human relationships. The girl Dido attracts him, not humanly, but as a symbol of their common freedom from 'human arms' (she succumbs to a cry for help, at the last, but for him there is only death, the supreme rejection). For this reason the play itself, for all its absorbing intellectual and psychological power (the power of egoism), is too bleak a symbol of life for some, and misses universal appeal. Both Flemyng and Wreford felt, in their study and playing of the part of the General, this slightly 'off-beat' view of life and expressed themselves on it in much the same words. 'These are not *real* characters in the ordinary theatre sense—or more importantly the *real life* sense. . . . I think this lack of minor humanities (which are of course the *major* ones) just prevents his being a *great* dramatist—but, of course, he may get this', wrote Wreford during the run. But a comment he also made, a personal one inspired by the play, I think crystallises one of the profound philosophical issues involved in the character of the General, and in the suggestion of which in this play Whiting does touch near-greatness: 'The "rightness for oneself", sometimes meaning "cruelty to others", is a perpetual theme', wrote Wreford, 'because immediately one recognises the repercussions of any action one realises that *all* action is dangerous—or potentially so. It is the desire to find defined limits which obviously concerns all thinking, feeling people.'

The drama of this play, which is a spiritual and mental drama, not truly an emotional one, concerns the fixing of these 'defined limits' according to individual conscience. It is, in the General's case, and to a lesser degree at the end in Dido's, an exercise in self-discovery, uncompromising, and also mystic. The Bristol press in varying degrees missed the play's stature and true nature ('haze of vapourings' was one of the more imbecile summings-up, and showed how completely out of touch even the Bristol Old Vic had been with thoughtful contemporary plays in the past). Neither critics nor public was ready for this one; but for the company there was much praise, especially for Wreford's 'commanding' portrayal of General Forster. 'By the restraint and control of his acting, it is possible to feel existing on the stage a man who has retreated within himself through the loneliness and confinement of prison life', wrote Peter Rodford, who did acknowledge something of the intellectual force of the play.

Michael Allinson's Cadmus was a clever assumption of distinguished senility, ironic, cynical, gently spoken in that beautifully clear (if perhaps slightly too young) diction that is the mark of the first-rate Shavian actor (Whiting's fine prose has something, indeed, of the Shavian clarity, structure and rhythm—admirable to speak and for all its weight of thought not difficult for actors to learn or hearers to follow). Mary Savidge as Catherine played with considerable emotional feeling, and Perlita Neilson as the girl Dido, too, subtly penetrated her hard shell in delicate moments of unexpected, expanding womanhood, strangely touching and preparing us for her capitulation in the last scene with Catherine. Paul Lee's drunken American had compassion as well as self-pity, a fine study of disintegration; and Ronald Hines as the young Captain of the last scene, though too sensitively neurotic and miscast, gave an interesting performance that made one wish to see him in further parts. He also had been in the London Old Vic company, but only at Bristol began to have a chance to show the makings of a very good actor.

Much Ado About Nothing, on October 19th, was received by harassed Bristolians with a sigh of relief; and a company far more harassed by this play than by *Marching Song* (two and a half weeks of rehearsal is far from ample for an elaborate Shakespearian production, and until near the opening night chaos was glumly anticipated) found themselves sweeping to success with a sparkling and responsive audience. John Moody's simplicity of production left both the Beatrice-Benedick and Claudio-Hero plots free to make their own natural effect, and though the Dogberry-Verges scenes still needed development, Paul Lee and Bruce Sharman, a mountainous cartoon and wisp of senility, proved specially popular later with the schoolchildren at matinée performances (Rodford considered this 'a masterful partnership', and Bushell engagingly noticed that Lee's Dogberry moved 'like an animated bell-tent'). The setting of Patrick Robertson was economic enough to satisfy the most rapacious Chancellor of the Exchequer: its architectural pillars with their hint of fan tracery were, in fact, made of white rope, but against deep blue backcloths the effect was often most pleasing, and the lighting seductive. Unfortunately the costumes in the main could not be specially designed; Rosemary Harris's were voluminous and most beautiful, but the Verona (Romeo period) caps and tights of the men were not perhaps ideal for this play, dispelling completely any sense of soldiers returning from war in the first scenes.

Nevertheless, Edgar Wreford gave the right forthright attack to Benedick's opening scenes, and his partnership with Rosemary Harris, newly come to Bristol to play Beatrice, was hailed as a success. 'They are as great a Beatrice and Benedick as we are ever likely to see in Bristol again—the authentic, vital, full-sized, scintillating pair that Shakespeare drew', wrote Bushell. 'How deliciously, and with what mischievous art, does this Beatrice deftly cross swords with the watchful Benedick, and how keen is his riposte!' And Rodford concurred: 'They look well in the parts, and well also do they play them. Perhaps they do trip too nippily over some of their exchanges, so that the wit of their badinage is occasionally understressed, but their playing, whether it is in moments of friendly cross-fire or earnest wooing, has a spontaneity and spirit, a dexterity and charm, that makes me wish now for the opportunity to compare them firing heavier guns in the battle of *The Taming of the Shrew.*'

Rosemary Harris was new to Shakespeare, but a young actress of exceptional beauty and quality who had deliberately sacrificed a budding career in the West End (where she had starred in *The Seven Year Itch*) in order to learn to play more serious work at the Bristol Old Vic. The twentieth-century touch was still discernible in her Beatrice, mainly in the speaking of the lines, but she moved with a floating grace and enchantingly combined mischief with ardour: her almond-shaped brown eyes widening in wonder—mirth quenched in a sudden melting radiance—as, hands clasped, she overheard the tale of Benedick's love. It was a touchingly youthful and completely warm response, the moment that will keep her Beatrice fresh in memory. Wreford, an actor hitherto cabined in character or middle-aged and elderly parts, responded with spirit and matched her in gaiety and tenderness ('Edgar's *bloomed*' murmured John Moody, with a twinkle, in the interval!), and his naturally serious training and temperament enabled him to play the Church scene, and the later challenge to Claudio, with unusual conviction. Benedick's essential worth and good nature were focused here; his face mirrored the shrewd suspicion of Don John as well as concern for Beatrice, obviously distressed for her cousin, and his 'I do love no one in the world as well as you—*Is not that strange?*' had a note of sudden wonder at the strange mystery of this emotion new to him—love.

Another notable performance was John Kidd's Leonato, a mature and convincing portrait which made us feel for Hero's father in the Church scene and after; and Ronald Hines's young Don John with a nervous facial 'tic', eloquently spoken, was an unexpected interpretation of a man brooding on and resentful of his bastardy, and unusually compelling. Michael Allinson played the Prince with style, and a newcomer, Edward Hardwicke, the young actor son of Sir Cedric Hardwicke and Helena Pickard, cleverly 'doubled' evil and good as Conrade and Friar Francis, displaying a good voice, incipient authority, and the ability to play a drunken scene realistically and without forcing (he was to show the same ability as the Marshal in the last scene of *The Crucible*). The darkly attractive John Cairney was Claudio (with a softly sung serenade), and Perlita Neilson Hero.

'It is a case of third time lucky', wrote *The Stage*, and the headlines unanimously glowed: 'Enchantment at Bristol Old Vic'—'Old Vic Hits Top Form'—'Much Ado—and About Something'. Audiences were equally responsive throughout the run.

The Crucible brought the London critics to Bristol for the first time this season, and the production received the attention of 'The Critics' programme on the B.B.C. Arthur Miller's sensational play—half melodrama, half tract on individual liberty and mass panic—came to England from New York and the alien setting of Salem, Massachusetts, during the eighteenth-century witchcraft scare and persecutions, fermented so powerfully on the Theatre Royal stage that the emotional impact was immediate. Miller's symbolic parallel was the witch-hunts of Senator McCarthy, but it is not a close parallel, and historically the Salem story—basically a true one—could stand on its own dramatic merits. It was a harrowing play, as vivid in its personal relationships as in its sense of the deadly infiltration of the personal grudge into a political autocracy once public hysteria and superstition have overthrown tolerance and commonsense; only in its last scene—the recantation and hanging of the hero, John Proctor, on a matter of conscience—did the author slacken the dramatic reins and tend to prolong and muffle his argument. Proctor's quibble on the reputation of his name was not large enough for the theme and unconvincing, although the scene of reconciliation with the wife was moving; and the escape of the girls whose spite and fear had caused all the trouble, though doubtless historical, made for dramatic shapelessness and inconclusiveness on the stage.

But until here Warren Jenkins's brilliant production, set against a background of lurid, thundery skies and overshadowing gibbet, kept up a sustained tension that was as remarkable as it was exciting, and from the company he obtained a magnificent response. It had not been an easy play to learn, for its language was the semi-biblical one of a puritan community, beautifully fashioned by Miller into a chiselled descriptiveness of phrase, graphic in metaphor and often poetic. Nearly all the parts, moreover, demanded immense power of emotional projection, sometimes collectively, sometimes individually. The full effect needed was orchestral and yet also highly visual, and Jenkins achieved wonders with his uplifted hands and rapt, ranting faces, his pulsing drumbeat and revivalist swaying in the scene with the negress Tituba, and the accumulative superstitious terror of the young girls in the trial. His actors, including several Bristol Old Vic School students, served him sensitively in these scenes ('Warren Jenkins is a superbly exciting producer', wrote Edgar Wreford during rehearsals) and the dramatic compulsion was such that the inevitable implausibility, to the twentieth-century mind, of this eighteenth-century religious atmosphere did not intrude in the theatre (a more calculated playing and production of the play later at the Royal Court Theatre in London lacked altogether the same impact—but it is essential to the period atmosphere).

Not merely the visiting London but also the Bristol critics registered the excitement generated by the play, and production and performance received wide admiration. 'This production in all its aspects—acting, lighting, settings, direction—sweeps the Bristol Old Vic up to the highest pinnacle of success. . . . Warren Jenkins directs it with masterly skill. Somehow he succeeds in making his audience share the terrors of the characters, and that is a tribute to him and also to the large cast who play it with such sincerity. Particularly would I pick out John Cairney's study of the priest, the seductive, vengeful Abigail of Pat Sandys, Perlita Neilson's pathetic servant girl robbed of her will-power by the fake fanaticism of Abigail, Mary Savidge's calm Rebecca and John Kidd's incisive Governor. And even above these, Edgar Wreford's tormented farmer, sacrificing himself in a vain endeavour to save his wife, played with quiet dignity by Rosemary Harris. A production which raises the Theatre Royal to a new dignity', wrote John Bennett.

'The Bristol Old Vic Company covers itself with distinction. Edgar Wreford and Rosemary Harris are particularly moving as the involved couple', concurred Alan Dent. 'The scene in the court-room in which, before the horrified eyes of the gullible and frightened judges, Abigail and her friends claim that they can feel the presence of the devil like a rushing, mighty wind is magnificently theatrical; and it is played by Miss Pat Sandys with assured diabolism, for all her frail appearance. Miss Sandys here looks as though she might well have trafficked with unmentionable things. Not all the players are as good as Miss Sandys. But Michael Allinson excellently catches the anguish of a man whose situation and profession force him to see guilt where no guilt is', wrote Harold Hobson. Peter Rodford thought the large cast 'dynamically led by Edgar Wreford, who apart from one or two unnecessary melodramatic gestures gave compelling force to his performance as the Salem farmer who dared to fight against the persecution'. 'Miss Rosemary Harris exactly catches the wan aridity of Proctor's wife', wrote Kenneth Tynan, 'and Miss Perlita Neilson and Mr. Paul Lee are perfect in lesser parts. . . . Mr. Patrick Robertson's settings, six gallows-trees shuffled to suggest roofs, doors and beams, brilliantly echo the play's theme.' 'The acting scorched our minds as it should, especially that of Edgar Wreford as a trapped farmer, Rosemary Harris as his wife— a steady, dignified performance that made me wish to see her as Hermione—Perlita Neilson as the terrified scrap of a girl whose nerve breaks, and Pat Sandys as the devilish Abigail. Naturally we expect a repertory cast to be versatile. Still, although I had met many of the Bristol company in other parts in other theatres, I was unprepared for quite so fierce a transformation as this. When curtain-fall released us to a November evening in King Street, Bristol, the shadows of Salem, 1692, were still about me.' This appreciation by J. C. Trewin (with its prophetic hint regarding Hermione) was supported by Cecil Wilson: 'When it does repeat its New York success in the West End, Perlita Neilson, Rosemary Harris, Pat Sandys, Edgar Wreford and Michael Allinson deserve to stay in the cast.'

The integrity and distinction of John Kidd's Judge Danforth, a fine and authoritative performance, were widely praised; but he is essentially a civilised actor and George Devine's harsher, more bigoted characterisation in London helped more to disperse the disbelief felt by some critics in the Judge's obstinate blindness to the truth (the difficulty, though, is in Miller's writing, and to an extent in our twentieth-century outlook on superstitions which even to intelligent eighteenth-century people could be terrifyingly real). Cairney's Rev. Parrish was weakened by his obvious youth and inexperience in a middle-aged part, and Abigail Williams, though played by red-haired Pat Sandys with arresting intensity, was a complex character, drawn by her suppressed passions to evil, which the actress did not quite fully explore (the conflict of calculating mind and dangerously unbalanced emotion, as well as the girl's sensuality, were brilliantly conveyed by Mary Ure in the Royal Court Theatre production). Otherwise the cast was without a flaw, and Paul Lee's gnarled octogenarian Giles Corey, as immovable as an oak but touchingly expressive in grief, was so fine a performance of a beautifully written part that when the character was omitted in the London production a hole seemed to be knocked into the human texture of the play. Phyllida Law and Ronald Hines as the bereaved puritans, Ann and Thomas Putnam, played minor parts with notable feeling and character-conviction, and among the students Annette Crosbie as the sick, frightened child Betty Parris, and Barbara Assoon as the negress Tituba, were outstanding. Patricia Healey, one of the other children, was in 1956 to score a success as the odious, neurotic schoolgirl, Mary, of Lillian Hellman's *Children's Hour* at the Arts Theatre.

T. C. Worsley in the *New Statesman and Nation* made an interesting comment which was a vindication of Moody's artistic policy: 'The Bristol Old Vic are to be congratulated on their enterprise in getting hold of and producing this play; and by doing so they remind us of one of the great gaps in our theatre arrangements. This play would find an enthusiastic audience in London, I believe, but it would be a limited one. Hopeless to drop it in, haphazard, somewhere round Shaftesbury Avenue on the off-chance that the people who might enjoy it would find it. They wouldn't—or they wouldn't, anyhow, in time. How badly we need an equivalent of the Old Vic or the Arts devoted to the modern repertory and run by someone with the enterprise and energy of, say, Mr. Anthony Quayle. There plays like this, or *Marching Song*, to take another example, could find their proper audience.'

Peter Ustinov's *No Sign of the Dove* on November 30th could be described as flood after storm, and its last-act Deluge with its prophetic latter-day Noah arrived appropriately in a West Country itself suffering from widespread inundation, and prone to ironic comment. The satire had failed in town after a run of eleven nights, and considering their abuse of *Marching Song* the Bristol critics were surprisingly mild—mild, in fact, as doves and even cooing. Ustinov's was much the inferior play, too frivolously mixing its satiric styles—from intellectual Bloomsbury to bedroom farce—and shattering its wisdom by the worthlessness of the characters. You cannot launch Jove's thunder against an erotic, posing *coterie*, and the symbol of the last-act flood, for all the Blake-like Matthew's fine speeches, misfires for lack of suitable targets. This world was not worth the drowning. But with a wittily colourful set (and striking last act on the rooftops) by Patrick Robertson, John Moody's production garnered the best in the play and much laughter besides, and Paul Lee gave a lovely performance as the ancient Matthew, reaching noble eloquence in the long final denunciation. Mary Savidge as Niobe D'Urt, Raymond Westwell (from Stratford-on-Avon) as her urbane brother, Michael Allinson and Phyllida Law did the best possible with the Bloomsbury set, while Edgar Wreford ('as admirable in assuming old age as he has been in the more virile characterisation of former productions', wrote *The Stage*) produced a rather disgruntled and shaggy German professor of libidinous habits and with an improbable resemblance to the pianist Paderewski.

Eleanor and Herbert Farjeon's musical play, *The Two Bouquets*, was chosen as the Christmas show. It was not to prove an ideal box-office choice owing to its lack of special appeal to children. Bristol playgoers, too, had become accustomed to seeing their favourites in a Christmas show specially written for them, and in spite of the introduction of a guest soprano, the pretty Catherine Hutchinson, and excellent tenor, Don Williams, to play Kate Gill and her lover Julian, the singing voices available were not equal—especially in the concerted numbers—to the musical demands of the score.

Yet the fact remains the play had more style and quality than the average Christmas concoction, it was produced gaily and prettily by Warren Jenkins in settings and costumes by Rosemary Vercoe (who cheerfully mixed her bustles and Edwardian blazers!), and many of the company were excellently fitted. John Cairney came into his own in a delightful study of diffidence as the shy Albert Porter, and Edgar Wreford gave a dashing impudence and charm to the scapegrace son, Edward Gill. He also sang his songs with great verve in a clear baritone, not too obviously incommoded by the fact that they were written for a tenor, until he lost his voice for a week in the middle of the run and handed the part over to Edward Hardwicke, who passed his first test as a leading player with flying colours. Mary Savidge and Paul Lee were the characteristic Victorian Mama and Papa Gill, with Phyllida Law as their niece Laura. Fanny Carby, another guest, brought tremendous gusto to the *soubrette* part of the actress Patty Moss and Michael Allinson as an actor, George, supported her with a moustache and ebullience equally unexpected.

Image in the Sun, the new play on February 8th, 1955, was written by Howard Clewes, the novelist, who had already had one play produced, *Quay South* (curiously enough, it had been presented at the Q Theatre under the management of Michael Allinson and his then partner, Margaret Ramsey). The new play was set in the hot sun of the Algerian town of Tipasa, built among the Roman ruins and a quiet centre of secret gun-running, and everything to do with atmosphere was finely suggested. Some of the inhabitants, too—the old cronies, Revau the innkeeper, Piquetot the Archaeologist, Beq the Gendarme—were well drawn, the dialogue was civilised and intelligent, the humour (including some butter-fingered comedy with explosives in the *Moon in the Yellow River* tradition and a wrongly-assumed demise) was engaging. It was a play about the inroads of progress which went awry technically in its main plot—for the leading character of the gun-runner Napier, a man burnt out by experience, and his hopeless romance with a young girl of the district, lacked full development in spite of a splendidly written scene between the man and his 'hound of justice', Captain Mathieu, who pursues him with an underlying feeling of comradeship and respect.

John Phillips, returned to the company to play Napier, was too quiet and essentially balanced and sane an actor to be able to put fire into the material where the author had failed; he was a good actor miscast, and the honours of the evening fell to Michael Allinson, who wore a French officer's uniform to the manner born and gave a beautifully integrated performance of a wise, dry charm. For once he held the critics—London and Bristol—in the palm of his hand, and dominated the play. John Cairney had a gentle and witty shot at the elderly archaeologist, and Rosemary Harris as his daughter played the last scene, after Napier's death, with poignant depth of feeling (somehow her scenes with Napier alive never quite caught fire). Paul Lee (in a clever make-up with the cunning, narrow eyes of a Van Gogh peasant) as Revau and Mary Savidge as his slatternly wife were excellent: her flat walk, spreading hips, were all part of a calculated middle-aged make-up and characterisation. Alfred Burke, formerly of the Birmingham Repertory, came as guest to play the gendarme, Beq, Edward Hardwicke and Bruce Sharman shone in the comedy of a Cockney chauffeur and demolition man, and Peter Wylde, who had been a fanatical Judge Haythorne in *The Crucible*, had a mild first chance at romance as the heroine's admirer, Bedou. John Moody produced a little too slowly and with insufficient variety of pace, but Patrick Robertson's settings were exotically beautiful, crumbling classical marble against a burning blue Algerian sky.

The Merchant of Venice on March 1st promised a new reading. John Moody in a programme note had written, wisely and rightly enough, 'This play has had more violence done to its essential unity than any of Shakespeare's plays'; but his suggestion that Antonio, not Shylock, was the principal character is borne out only to a degree by the nature of the plot, and not at all in the dramatic business of the play, where Shylock as a stage character appears altogether richer, fuller in detail and dynamic in effect. It was Shakespeare, the artist and humanist, once again at work on the bare bones of a plot, and although Moody could and did do much, in his production, to restore the unity and give Antonio his due place (partly by placing an interval as the Merchant gazed sadly after Bassanio's departing ship), he still could not prevent this Shylock from thrusting more conclusively into one's interest.

This was in no way due to a cleavage of view between actor and producer, for Wreford was absolutely at one with Moody in deprecating any romanticism of the part or bid to win sympathy. He played him as he believed the text demanded, with great integrity and without 'actor's frills'—as a robust, vindictive, round-shouldered, gloatingly humorous figure, rich but ugly, zestful in evil, and a target of our laughter, not pity, at the hasty departure in the trial: 'I am not well . . .' The interpretation succeeded remarkably well: it was a fine one with an effective Hebraic make-up (Wreford, once a draughtsman and designer, had sketched some magnificent preliminary 'heads'), not overdoing the comedy but encouraging it to spring spontaneously from the lines. The hair was red not in the eighteenth-century comic tradition but dark auburn streaked with grey. Strong of voice, oriental of gesture, he lacked variety in the first scene and pressed vocally a little too hard, but thereafter made his points with the mixture of full-blooded gusto and subtlety of detail that is characteristic of all the best Shylocks. But there were no concessions; 'I had it of Leah' made its point of grief but it was not dwelt on, the relationship with the daughter who hates him never sentimentalised. This was 'a hearty, almost sportive fellow, managing the bond business like a joke to be retold later with great relish at the club', in Bushell's words (and of course the text supports it). But the humour was dangerous, hatred spurting out of it. 'Shylock, not the Merchant, still dominates the play', was John Coe's headline, and he added: 'Mr. Wreford's Shylock in repose looked like a Hebrew prophet: the make-up was perfect. When he was in full spate it was the force of his revengeful temper and his natural pride that captured our attention. This was as powerful a Shylock as any I have seen since the war.'

Nevertheless, the play's unities *were* preserved: Moody's careful direction with its swift changes from Venice to Belmont showed us the skill with which Shakespeare balances the two plots as they slowly converge to meet in the trial; the romance was duly starred; and Michael Allinson's quietly noble Antonio helped greatly in fastening our interest on his personal loneliness and problem. There could have been more gaiety, and it was certainly a strange mistake to dress Gratiano and the young bloods of Venice in black like a bunch of Hamlets, but nothing was distorted. Robertson's settings—with permanent side-buildings in red brick—were not the prettiest imaginable but his use of back-cloth gauzes switched us from Venice to Belmont and back in a series of magical flashes, and Rosemary Harris's fairy princess Portia, mischievous and ardent, gave an enchantment to all her scenes. Perlita Neilson, now in command of her voice, was a charming Nerissa, witty without loss of grace; John Humphry (new to Bristol though he was to return the following season) looked handsome and spoke with increasing eloquence as Bassanio; Paul Lee doubled Arragon with an imposing, beautiful-voiced Duke of Venice; Bruce Sharman made Young Gobbo a tawny-haired likeable Cockney, freshening a hackneyed part; Phyllida Law was a red-haired Jessica of spirit; and Edward Hardwicke as her Lorenzo showed a growing feeling for verse. Cairney's

The Enchanted (Giraudoux), 1955. Rosemary Harris as Isabelle and
Michael Allinson as the Supervisor.

ABOVE: *The Confidential Clerk* (T. S. Eliot), 1955. L. *to* R. Mary Savidge as Lady Elizabeth, Rosemary Harris as Lucasta, Ronald Hines as B. Kaghan.

BELOW: *The Mulberry Bush* (Angus Wilson), 1955. L. *to* R. John Cairney as Kurt Landeck, Derek Godfrey as James Padley and Mary Hinton as Rose Padley.

Both photos by Desmond Tripp

The Winter's Tale, 1955. Perlita Neilson as Perdita and Edward Hardwicke as Florizel.

The Crucible (Arthur Miller), 1954. Edgar Wreford (centre) as John
Proctor, Rosemary Harris as Elizabeth Proctor and John Cairney
as the Rev. Parris.

gaunt, arresting Scots face was not ideal for Gratiano and the black costume doubtless further subdued him, but Ronald Hines stood out notably as Salerio, bringing his sad news to Belmont with a musical dignity and grave ease.

These last young actors were responsible also for the two Bristol Old Vic babies of the season: Deborah Hines, born on January 17th, 1955, and Jennifer Cairney, born on February 19th.

Smaller-than-expected audiences for *The Merchant* may have been influenced by a rather limp television production (with ex-Bristol Vic players Laurence Payne and Jane Wenham alone scintillating as Gratiano and Nerissa) which coincided with its first week; but there was ample recompense with Jean Giraudoux's *The Enchanted*, the English version of *Intermezzo*, which as at the Arts Theatre the previous summer played to packed houses and proved astonishingly (for it is a delicate, subtle and satiric play) to English taste. It opened on March 29th, 1955, and less than a week later Edgar Wreford was able to write that it 'seems to be setting a record for business already'. 'It was a very good first night', he wrote, '—full house and with the company really ready and eager to give a performance with an audience. It went very well indeed—not a hitch, I think. . . . It's lovely to do and the "production" is proving its worth.'

Indeed the company as well as the audience were specially happy with this play, and in spite of a disappointingly unmagical set by Patrick Robertson, Frank Dunlop, the young producer, won the special admiration of his actors and preserved a notable balance between mystery, romance and satire. Dunlop had been a production student of the Old Vic Dramatic School and he seemed to have absorbed the Byam Shaw gift of imparting a consistent 'style' and feeling to his acting team. 'Above all it was Frank Dunlop, the producer, with an imaginative talent of which I hope we shall see more, who guided this remarkable little play between Scylla and Charybdis to a safe landing', wrote John Coe.

The play, wrote Louis Jouvet, for whose company Giraudoux wrote it, 'is the biography of a moment in the life of a young girl—when she turns from girlhood to womanhood'. It is a fantasy of the spiritual call of death which is defeated only by the exorcism of the fascinating ghost who calls her, and the lure of life as propounded, in a sudden firework display of wit, by a more prosaic young civil servant. But it is a comedy, too, with an almost Gilbertian topsy-turvydom in its local-government satire, and its radiance is one of happiness as well as the mystery of life and the soul. The sense of 'mystery' was centred, at Bristol, not merely in the Ghost of John Cairney but in the Doctor of Edgar Wreford, who conjured the unknown forces—a link between the two worlds of the play—with an unexpectedly sensitive grasp of the *fey* and a gently ironic compassion: one of his finest performances at Bristol. But the pivot is still the heroine, Isabel, in which Rosemary Harris in a striped dress and picture hat looked quite breathtakingly beautiful, and played with a warm, inner radiance and poignancy of feeling that illumined the whole play. 'This sort of part might have been written for Rosemary Harris, who brings to it a delicate air of enchantment and an underlying sense of fun that are quite irresistible', wrote Coe. 'Few of our contemporary actresses know how to deal with fantasy. Miss Harris is never worried by the many pitfalls that lie in wait for her.'

The dressing of the play nearer its own period (1911) gave the story a charm not quite captured in the modern-dress production of the French company of Jean-Louis Barrault seen in England later, and indeed only in two cases did Barrault's company equal or surpass the English ones: his own copper-tongued, unearthly, rather sinister Ghost and Jean Desailly's Supervisor of Weights and Measures, which showed how much this whole part and especially his famous last-act speech on the enchantments of Civil Service life gain from the French style of acting and the French language. No translation can capture its essential *panache*, but Michael Allinson substituted a praiseworthy English elegance, volubility and charm. Ronald Hines, in his first major part as the Inspector officially disapproving of a Ghost, 'gives a reading of the part that just falls short of being a brilliantly authoritative one', wrote Coe; Perlita Neilson, as at the Arts Theatre, charmingly led the chorus of little girls (the one marked out for Isabel's future on reaching womanhood), Mary Savidge and Phyllida Law made hits as the rather overdrawn cackling old maids, Paul Lee dithered as the Mayor, and Edward Hardwicke and Antony Tuckey delivered the Executioners' masonic creed with a lovely solemnity and aplomb.

A new play had been announced for the following production, but in the event Moody chose Denis Johnston's comedy *The Golden Cuckoo*, which had been revised since its brief London production before the war. It is a tale of typically Irish humour, founded on an authentic incident of the storming of a village post office, and with a brilliantly eccentric chief character of an elderly distinguished journalist, Mr. Dotheright, whose fight for justice over what many would consider a trifle of underpayment brings him to the lunatic asylum but not to relinquishment of his cause. It is a warming and wonderful character to play (in Dublin, a year later, it was acted by Cyril Cusack), but Paul Lee, against all one's expectations, just failed to bring to it the necessary touch of eccentricity and hint of genuine tragedy, although his performance was gentle and touching within its range. The other parts are colourful 'types' rather than characters, and from the heap of talent available only John Cairney, as Mr. Hooley, a refractory cabman, emerges vividly in memory. It is a play of fun and wisdom, which reads most amusingly, but its essence is Irish humour and John Moody lost some of it by de-localising his atmosphere. There was a bright and clever first-act expressionistic set of Dotheright's home by Peter Snow, but although they played cleverly the company never felt really happy in the play.

The Winter's Tale was an odd choice, not because it is not a more enchanting play than many Bristolians had realised, but because there was no one in the company who in temperament and experience was an obvious choice for Leontes—a difficult part at best, requiring the jealous passion of an Othello as well as the anguish and hatred of what we would now doubtless ascribe to a 'mixed-up kid' mentality. After some hesitation Michael Allinson was chosen, and he made a good attempt at darkening evil and played the last scenes of remorse and reconciliation most movingly, but without ever convincing us that he carried the necessary emotional guns. He is, in fact, essentially a civilised and elegant actor, best in dry charm of which Leontes has no trace. He was not helped by a very slow, bare, undramatic production of the first scenes, though Moody later made amends with a fairy-like transformation to Bohemia, in a shower of will-o'-the-wisp lights like snowflakes, conjured by Allinson himself behind the mask of Time, the chorus. The 'statue' scene too was appealing in its candle-lit serenity, and here both the Leontes and Rosemary Harris's lovely, sorrowing Hermione came to artistic fulfilment.

Mary Savidge was a splendid Paulina, gentler than usual, who could have played a moving Hermione, Edgar Wreford a lusty,

gay, gypsy-skinned rogue Autolycus, Paul Lee the most warmly
human Old Shepherd I can remember (an exquisite performance),
John Cairney his son, Antony Tuckey—in one of his rare good
parts—a moving and notably spoken Camillo, and Ronald Hines
a more than usually intelligent and eloquent Polixenes. And in the
sheep-shearing scenes Perlita Neilson and Edward Hardwicke, as
Perdita and Florizel, were as good to look on as to listen to; a
spring-like younger generation come to disperse the frosts of
their elders' strife. By an original but not unwise stroke of casting Perlita Neilson also played the other ill-starred child of
Leontes and Hermione, the boy Mamillius. The dances of Elizabeth
West added charm and buoyancy to the country scenes, in which
the production was wholly successful.

Only a nucleus of the company remained after *The Winter's
Tale* and was concentrated in a remarkably fine performance of
T. S. Eliot's *The Confidential Clerk*, produced on May 30th with
a much-admired sense of balance by André Van Gyseghem, and
designed brilliantly by Patrick Robertson, whose pent-house was
both picturesque and livable-in and who conceived the Mulhammer
library as a decorative Wedgwood reflection of Sir Claude's taste
for pottery. Only Peter Rodford was doubtful about the play: the
general reception was one of delight, and the acting throughout
most beautifully and sensitively realised the wisdom lurking
beneath the farcical plot.

Mary Savidge's smart, poised, scatter-brained but essentially
warm and affectionate Lady Elizabeth was one of her triumphs of
the season: an exercise in high comedy that never unbalanced
the play. Edgar Wreford's Sir Claude, finely made up as a distinguished rather than ebullient tycoon of advanced middle age,
was drily humorous but also deeply responsive to the inward
frustration ('a man', wrote Rodford, 'with impressive bearing
and—most important this—a human heart'); Rosemary Harris
was mischievously enchanting as Lucasta, a part she had already
played at the Paris Festival and on tour, without loss of moving
quality in the tender scene with Colby; Michael Allinson, a little
mannered, responded sensitively in this scene; Paul Lee was
naturally cast as the elderly Eggerson, in which Alan Webb had
been so delightful in town; Ronald Hines, excellent in his
comedy timing, made B. Kaghan an attractive, down-to-earth
young man, with a shrewd human understanding under the

banter; and Phyllida Law triumphed over youth in a remarkable portrait of middle-aged suburban respectability as Mrs. Guzzard.

You and Your Wife, too, had a small cast and no part for Rosemary Harris, and it was inevitable the last play of the season should therefore have for the audience a rather depleted air. Produced on June 28th, this new domestic comedy by Denis Cannan had a slight surface of divorce-court misunderstandings but dialogue which was often both witty and philosophically wise. The warring couples were played by Michael Allinson, Peggy Simpson, Mary Savidge and Paul Lee (at last appearing as an attractive man only a few years older than himself, doubtless to the astonishment of many Bristolian admirers who had come to associate him with the longevity of Noah). All of them distinguished themselves in the modern arguments and style, although Allinson, finely voluble as a red-bearded intellectual who has discovered rather late the joys of 'connubialism', had a potentially excellent part which disappointingly faded later. Gillian Lewis, a Bristol Vic student, had her first prominent part as the younger heroine and looked pretty and played with assurance. Ronald Hines was her attractive opposite, John Cairney gave a delightful study of an elderly dispenser of philosophic clichés, and Edgar Wreford, in the play's best character part, brought a rich Cockney accent and Dickensian gusto and detail to an unreformable escaped convict named Goich.

It was not the ideal choice for an end-of-season production nor, though it played amusingly, a very successful play, but it showed the excellent standard of style and teamwork the company could now attain (Peggy Simpson, the guest, slipped neatly into the team) and made it seem all the more regrettable that none of the leading players (except Edgar Wreford, who for his own reasons refused, and John Cairney, who accepted) were invited to return. T. C. Worsley was wholly captivated by the play and praised the company and author for 'an evening of unalloyed pleasure. Lucky Bristol! Or, rather, not lucky, but sensible Bristol, to find for themselves and enjoy such a treat!'

It was a cheerful and appreciative note on which to end an ambitious season, which began better than it ended, did not always use available talent to full advantage, but had matched high endeavour with achievement in many cases.   [A.W.]

CHAPTER TWELVE

The Eleventh Season
1955 *to* 1956

IN THE ELEVENTH SEASON, which marked the end of the first ten years of the Bristol Old Vic Company, there were three episodes which deserve to be recorded.

To take them in their reverse order—at the end of the season there came the opening of the handsome new school premises. Dame Sybil Thorndike and Sir Lewis Casson, aged seventy-four and eighty respectively, and recently returned from a two-year world tour, slipped down gaily to Bristol in between two performances at the Phoenix Theatre. As guests of honour, they were happy to recall their earlier connections with the Theatre Royal. The official opening should have been performed by the Lord Mayor, Alderman Watson Allan, who had for some years been a member of the Bristol Old Vic management committee. To his great regret he was unable to be present; but the Corporation was well represented by his colleague Alderman Chamberlain, who, as chairman of the school committee, had been so largely responsible for the adaptation and equipment of the building.

In June the company paid their second visit to Zürich—this time with *The Rivals*. Again the hospitality was overwhelming—it included a trip by mountain railway to the snow-clad peaks of Mount Pilatus, where in the centrally heated hotel an incredible meal was served. The centre of attraction both on stage and off was, of course, Moira Shearer, and may I here pay my tribute to Miss Shearer. The social position of the leading lady of the company is always a difficult one. In all my thirty-five years' managerial experience I have never seen it handled with such effortless grace and natural charm as it was on this occasion by Moira Shearer. In that foreign land she was a joyous and distinguished ambassadress both of the theatre and of her country.

On Saturday, February 18th, the tenth anniversary of the Bristol Old Vic was celebrated. (The actual date should have been the 19th, but this fell on a Sunday.) The play was *King Lear* and the attempt was made to gather in as many old friends as possible. Hugh Hunt sent a cable from Australia, and from his Bristol company came Yvonne Mitchell, Jill Balcon and Guy Sheppard. Denis Cannan represented the company which had been led by Allan Davis. Denis Carey was present, and with him came Laurence Payne and Pamela Alan. Christopher Hassall, who had written the prologue for the opening performance in 1946, wrote a fresh version which was beautifully spoken by Yvonne Mitchell, who had played the part of Cherry in that first production of *The Beaux' Stratagem*. The main speech was made by Michael MacOwan, now head of the London Drama School, L.A.M.D.A., and who, in 1946, had been the drama director of the Arts Council, responsible for the establishment of the company. He was good enough to refer to me as the godfather of the company, and he went on to say that such enterprises were the roots from which the whole of the British theatre gained sustenance. Without them there could be no theatrical profession. 'When roots are planted as firmly as this, everyone who comes here cannot help but draw strength from them.'

And on that note we can perhaps sum up. The Bristol Old Vic Company has in its ten years nobly fulfilled the dual functions of every repertory—the provision of entertainment for the local citizens and the training of artists on their way to the Metropolis. It has had wise guidance, notably from that wit and humanist, Sir Philip Morris, and it has stood in the forefront of the repertory movement of its time. Moreover, it has helped to give that movement a new importance in the national theatre. Gradually public taste is changing. The metropolitan theatre, after the first six weeks' run of any play, has always depended largely on its provincial visitors. That provincial audience, in the postwar decade, has increasingly supported its own repertory theatres, and by so doing has acquired a taste for the 'team' rather than for the 'star'. Naturally the star will always attract, but events of the last few years have shown that there is a public in London today (which in the last decade there was not) who need no other attraction but the play and 'the team'. *Salad Days* might be written off as an exception, but when it is flanked by the successes of *The Boy Friend*, *Sailor Beware*, *Waiting for Godot* and *Cranks*, all of them 'starless', and all emanating from repertory or experimental theatres, then this surely indicates a trend. For the creation of this new interest in the 'team', perhaps no man has been more responsible than Denis Carey.

Finance has the final word—since 1942 the avaricious jaws of the eighteenth-century building have swallowed up a vast amount of money from the Arts Council, the Bristol Corporation, as well as all the profits made by C.E.M.A. during the war years. £72,000 have been spent on the maintenance of the 'ancient monument'. The Bristol Old Vic Company, however, has paid its way, and has in the first ten years of its existence made, in all, just under £1,000 profit.   [c.l.]

John Moody's second season opened lightly with Thornton Wilder's *The Matchmaker* on September 5th, 1955. John Cairney, Phyllida Law and Edward Hardwicke alone remained after the clean sweep of the previous season: none of them yet top-rankers, although Phyllida Law had this time (through the illness of Peggy Simpson, who was engaged for it) a leading part, that of the warm-hearted milliner, Mrs. Molloy, which Eileen Herlie had acted with such an enchanting sense of comedy at the Haymarket Theatre, and which the ex-Bristol student now played 'with a sparkling, heart-warming sense of the fun and feeling written into it'.

The chief role, that of Mrs. Levi (played by the striking comedienne Ruth Gordon in town), was given to a guest actress, Jessie Evans, already known at Bristol, and other former Bristol Old Vic actors who now returned for the season were Eric Porter, Alan Dobie and John Humphry, the tall young Tennent actor who had made an attractive single appearance as Bassanio the previous season. Outstanding among the newcomers was Derek Godfrey, a product of the Byam Shaw Old Vic Dramatic School, who had played leading parts for two seasons at the Nottingham Repertory and had formerly been with the Stratford-on-Avon Shakespeare Company and the Salisbury Arts Theatre (where he played Hamlet). He had only a small part, Malachi Stack, in *The Matchmaker*, but was to take leading character parts shortly. Peter O'Toole, a young R.A.D.A. student who had won an H. M. Tennent award and was great-nephew of the famous Irish actor and friend of Irving, J. L. Toole, was engaged for small parts which were to rise spectacularly the following season, when he played the major part of the Pope in the American play about

The Skin of Our Teeth (Thornton Wilder), 1956. Moira Shearer as Sabina and Derek Godfrey as Mr. Antrobus.

ABOVE: *King Lear*, 1956. Eric Porter as King Lear and Moira Shearer as Cordelia, with Joseph O'Conor (left background) as Kent.

BELOW: *The Empty Chair* (Peter Ustinov), 1956. L. *to* R. foreground. Michael Meachum (St. Just), John Humphry (Barras), Alan Dobie (Robespierre) and Phyllida Law (Mme Danton).

Both photos by Desmond Tripp

Galileo, *The Lamp at Midnight*. Sonia Fraser, an Assistant Stage Manager from the Bristol School, played the milliner's assistant, Minnie Fay, and John Cairney's pretty young wife, Sheila Cowan, the merchant's romantic daughter. Viola Lyel, a clever actress of long experience at the Old Vic and Stratford, joined the company until Christmas and played the eccentric aunt Flora Van Huysen. Moira Shearer, the new Bristol Old Vic leading lady, did not appear until the production of *Ondine* in October.

The company in the circumstances could only give a scrappy indication of its eventual team quality, and one headline proclaimed a 'Dull Play but a Good Company'. Many would disagree about the play, though it is not an original Wilder work, being founded on his earlier *The Merchant of Yonkers*, which in its turn derived from European plays. Its technique, however, is assured and takes the audience in its confidence in an individual use of soliloquy and 'asides', and the story has a certain charm—more in the case of the Irish milliner's romance than that of the matchmaker and the merchant themselves, which lean heavily on the guns of personality fired by Mrs. Levi. Jessie Evans had an inevitable success—'a beautifully observed piece of comedy in the robust tradition', wrote Coe. 'It was illuminated with a wealth of amusing gesture and intonation and carried forward on a tide of bustling attack. Opposite her, Eric Porter, whose return to the Old Vic after a full year's absence is as important as it was necessary, made an excellent foil as the irascible merchant Vandergelder.' John Humphry joined Phyllida Law as the male half of the Irish milliner's romance, and as Cornelius Hackle, the clerk who breaks his bonds and sets out for a spree in New York, he showed the charm of shyness and a gay and easy comedy touch (which was to illumine later his delightful Gratiano in *The Merchant of Venice* at the Old Vic). Cairney supported him as his timid partner in painting the town red. Alan Dobie played the fairly unrewarding part of the artist who woos the merchant's daughter, and Moody produced with settings by Patrick Robertson.

Angus Wilson's first play, *The Mulberry Bush*, on September 27th, brought honour to the Bristol Old Vic management for being the first to present it and inevitably aroused wide national interest. The introduction of good literary brains into the theatre is a problem of the British stage: financially, such are the hazards of the production of serious plays in our commercial West

End theatre, the writer of literary talent is discouraged, a situation not comparable in France, which as a result has an altogether richer intellectual theatre. Mr. Wilson's play, somewhat revised, was later produced in London as the opening production of the English Stage Society at the Royal Court Theatre on April 2nd, 1956, but to Bristol goes first honour and on the whole a better-acted production. A picture of academic life, with two elderly liberals whose life of good social works has not produced any real understanding of living individuals and the younger generations, it is a play of literary penetration and purpose which just evades dramatic success because its characters are too coldly analysed for plausibility or winning sympathy, and we are told more about them in the words of others than through their own personal life on the stage.

It may be possible that Wilson drew them too seriously and they might have responded better to the satiric touch which is his more normal approach in his novels; as it is they sometimes exasperate, only rarely move, and it is an arguable question whether the comic touch of Viola Lyel, the actress, and André Van Gyseghem, the producer, was quite what was needed for the character of the dead son's mistress, Mrs. Loughton-Moore.

Nevertheless, the feeling persisted that a new mind of notable distinction had entered the theatre. Patrick Robertson gave the play a beautiful collegiate garden setting in the second act, and several of the cast gave fine performances: most notably Mary Hinton, a guest player, as the elderly liberal Rose Padley. This was acting of true humanity, detailed understanding and a tragic edge, by an actress the right age for the part. Inevitably in the circumstances the thirty-one-year-old Derek Godfrey as her husband could not quite plausibly match her in an assumption of age, although he is one of our finest young actors of middle and old age when not cruelly put up against the real thing. His quiet, distinguished touch, however, was helpful. Eric Porter for once played a younger character, Peter Lord, not very interestingly, the fine actress Marie Ney did her best with the daughter gallantly dying of cancer, John Humphry was her son, a weak drunkard, and Yvonne Furneaux the granddaughter, Ann Padley, who is most moved by realisation of her father's history. More obviously effective character work was allotted to Alan Dobie as the down-at-heel Captain Wallcott and to John Cairney as the Padleys' insufferable displaced German protégé, Kurt Landeck—the last a nasty example of mixed-up youth masquerading as genius which no actor could make wholly credible, but which Cairney's striking dark tousled appearance excellently fitted. Phyllida Law also put up a gallant fight as another mixed-up kid of adolescent but tearing emotional indiscipline, to which her classic features and entire histrionic personality were combustibly ill-suited.

Giraudoux's *Ondine* was written six years after *The Enchanted*, which had been a major success the previous season. Its theme is more obviously magical—the story of a water-nymph who loves a mortal knight with a depth and changelessness outside his human capability, a fact which brings tragedy to both after a second act of Giraudoux's special brand of original satire. Ondine in her fishing hut—the changeling daughter of an aged peasant couple—is a creature of fire and air, caprice and affection; in the last act, caught in the toils of a fishing net and on trial for her life, she is one of still-glowing sacrificial love and tragedy. But in the second, the innocent at Court, she must have an elegant feeling for wit and satiric comedy and in this act particularly Moira Shearer was volubly delightful. In spite of her porcelain beauty and pastel lyricism as a dancer, on the speaking stage she is not so closely attuned to this part as its nymph-like nature might suggest. She has a hard metal of Scots brain, a keen wit, a voice soft but crystalline as a Highland stream, feeling rather than *depth* of feeling, a lightness and precision of approach in which an excellent technique is not yet ready to be submerged in the abandon of emotion.

All this gave a special quality to her Ondine and proclaimed a distinctive actress who might well find her natural element in the Lady Teazles of eighteenth-century comedy, and in the second act of this Giraudoux play more than the last and moments of the first. Wide-eyed, in a wig like blonde flowing seaweed (it was cut to a better length after the first night), she was enchanting with a rather surface enchantment, witty, cool, engagingly affectionate. The deeper notes of ardent womanhood, the tragic immolation of the close, escaped her. Nevertheless, an actress not known to be a former ballerina and new (apart from Titania) to the dramatic stage would have won a greater triumph in this part and her later ones at Bristol than Miss Shearer was allowed by some critics, who approached her performances with an obvious bias and in some cases a certain wrong-headedness. For what Moira Shearer lacked as yet was not, as they assumed, technique, but the ability after years of training in the highly disciplined art of ballet to *forget* technique and let the emotion within her (as it is deep within us all) fling itself spontaneously free. That some depth and force of feeling was there her Cordelia was later to show. In the meantime, her Ondine was bewitching, witty, sometimes touching and always sincere, and a feat of memory more experienced actresses might envy.

Giraudoux's play is a beautiful one with a symbol of earthly aspiration which is clear and true, but only the most delicate touch can save its throne-room and legal satire from breaking it in two. John Moody's Old Vic production, rather fussily dressed by ballet designer Nicholas Georgiadis but with a distressingly bare last act, succeeded only in part, although several performances were distinctive and the music of Henri Sauguet was used. Porter was outstanding as the King sensitive to the wart on his nose and charmed from his tetchy sensitivity by Ondine's unsophisticated candour; John Humphry made a stalwart and nicely puzzled hero-knight and Alan Dobie a dignified and mysterious King of the Ondines; Derek Godfrey and Peter O'Toole attracted attention as Lord Chamberlain and Superintendent of the Theatre; Viola Lyel was a true moving peasant as Ondine's supposed mother and Edward Hardwicke achieved an interesting double as her father and a slightly gormless young fisherman. Maurice Valency's adaptation was used, and included some telescoping of characters.

Uncle Vanya on November 8th continued John Moody's instinct for the comedy in Tchehov, which Rodford felt got 'out of hand' in the climax to the third act, Vanya's attempt to shoot the Professor. But Eric Porter as Vanya was inclined to be too strenuous and assured, and to miss the irresolute eccentricity of the character, which made the effect of his missing at short range in any case beyond the limits of reasonable comedy. It was, wrote Rodford, 'a solid piece of acting, enhanced by many a shrewd and meaningful shrug'; but solidity is just the quality the Tchehovian Uncle Vanyas do not possess, and this excellent actor might indeed have been better cast as Astrov, the frustrated yet idealistic and practical doctor who can bloom with sombre magnificence in the hands of a fine actor, as Laurence Olivier showed in a definitive

Old Vic production. John Humphry, 'aloof and immaculately dressed', is a painstaking and highly intelligent young actor, but his youth could not quite grasp at Astrov's embittered maturity, nor could it be expected to do so at this stage in his career, and the same inevitably applied to Phyllida Law's Marya Voynitsky. Derek Godfrey, on the other hand, made a brilliant Professor. 'Derek Godfrey's egotistical old fraud of a professor was full of compelling detail, and Moira Shearer, his young wife, succeeded admirably in looking too bored to stand up—only to reveal a surprising warmth of humanity when she suddenly opened her heart to pity and, momentarily, to love', wrote the *Western Daily Press*. Rodford, too, noted her beautiful dresses and poised acting. Her voice, perhaps, was still too crystalline—and her mind too shrewd—for the animal indolence of Yelena, though she was suited to it in many ways and rose unexpectedly to the final moving scene alone. She would have been readier for the part later in the season, and felt the limitation herself.

Sonia Fraser, a delicate actress from the School, was a natural Sonia, touching and admired. 'Sonia Fraser's final renouncement and elegy of faith had all the passion of a liturgy—a Nunc Dimittis that became a Magnificat', wrote the *Western Daily Press*. Equally successful was Alan Dobie's impoverished Telyegin. 'Of Telyegin', wrote Coe, 'Alan Dobie made a telling cameo. Here was unquestioned acceptance of destiny. Mr. Dobie should go very far in the theatre.' Viola Lyel's authentic old nurse Marina completed the cast. Nicholas Georgiadis designed the cut-out style of settings, with a garden criticised for its 'flat and gloomy appearance'.

The flamboyant scherzo of Ben Jonson's *Volpone* followed the muted strings of Tchehov's *Uncle Vanya*. Produced on November 29th, it was the expected triumph for Eric Porter as the Fox ('pulling out all the stops', as Peter Rodford wrote), and a minor one, less expected, for Derek Godfrey in a brilliant caricature of Voltore, the Vulture at the bed of the (presumed) dying Miser. Antony Tuckey as Corbaccio, the Raven, and Peter O'Toole as Corvino, the Crow, supported Godfrey, with Alan Dobie as a subtle and rather lightweight Mosca, a black Fly in sideboards. The version, unlike that frequently performed by Donald Wolfit in London, included the satire of the British travellers abroad, Sir Politick and Lady Would-Be, played amusingly by John Humphry ('a splash of sartorial elegance topped by a sort of yellow pith-helmet') and Viola Lyel. Moira Shearer was the distressed and ill-used heroine Celia (her vicissitudes included a broken finger from a violent scene with Volpone during the run), and Edward Hardwicke a vigorous young hero, Bonario.

It was inevitable that Porter's large-size performance of the great classical part should be the centre of interest. 'Mr. Porter's reading of Volpone missed nothing of the character's stupendous spivvery. In him arch-roguery was enthroned. Watch, too, how Mr. Porter acts with his whole body, how he makes a point merely by crooking a finger.' This was the general view, and the only criticism was of Jonson's own metaphorical error: 'his Volpone has a lion's mane and a lion's roar that can hardly be reconciled with the sly cunning of a fox. But that is Jonson's mistake, not Mr. Porter's, for no fox ever acted with such roguish delight or lecherous intent as does Volpone'. It isn't quite true—Volpone has fox-like cunning to spare—but it is true that the part, as Wolfit has shown, needs and responds to an actor of 'size'.

The play was the first to be produced at Bristol by John Harrison, the adventurous young producer of the Nottingham Playhouse Theatre, who stressed the allegorical quality of the story in a production described as 'slick and full-blooded', with a vivid emphasis on bird-like poses and movements in the characters of the Vulture, Raven and Crow, which came to a striking climax in the court scenes when Godfrey as Voltore, the advocate, spread his arms wide like a vulture about to swoop on the defendants.

For Christmas this year Bristol chose V. C. Clinton-Baddeley's *Dick Whittington*. Moira Shearer had been intended to play Principal Boy, but feeling Gavin Gordon's music when it arrived too demanding for an amateur singer she relinquished the part to the charming and experienced Betty Huntly-Wright, and retired to study if not entirely to rest (indefatigable in her desire to learn and gain experience, she did actually appear for one week during the run of the pantomime as a singer among the chorus—her red hair carefully disguised so that she was not 'spotted' by the audience!). The pantomime proved as always much to Bristol taste, being written specially for the company, and Phyllida Law distinguished herself by designing the costumes (which 'alone', wrote John Coe, 'make a visit to this show worth while') as well as playing the parts of Sally and a Roedeanian Britannia. Eric

Porter was a highly successful 'Dame' Cicely Suett, in ringlets and gingham, Alan Dobie a 'light-footed' Cat, John Cairney emerged (among other things) gorgeously turbaned as a Sultan, John Humphry was King Rat, Elizabeth West (who again arranged the dances) a White Cat, and Derek Godfrey doubled the pompous Alderman Fitzwarren with 'a King Neptune vaguely reminiscent of Billy Russell'. Margot Anderson was the 'guest' Principal Girl, Peter O'Toole and Edward Hardwicke collected several parts apiece, and Lally Bowers was the presiding coupleteer, Fairy Snowflake.

Eric Porter might well have chosen to 'rest' during the Christmas pantomime, for his next Herculean task was King Lear, chosen to mark the Bristol Old Vic's tenth anniversary and produced on February 14th, 1956.

This was, in my view (I saw it in company with Rosemary Harris, equally impressed and deeply moved, at a matinée during its last week), the finest production John Moody had yet directed and in every way and by any Shakespearian standards an outstanding achievement which brought honour to the Bristol Old Vic. It is surprising to find the local critics, after the first performance, were comparatively unimpressed (Rodford in addition complained of the full version acted and wished Moody had cut the sub-plot and concentrated more on Lear, a view quickly challenged by correspondents in the Press). Yet it was Moody's very insistence on leaving Shakespeare to make his own constructional impact that gave the production such balance, brought out the special character and allegory of the 'double' plot of two fathers suffering through their own sins and their own children, and showed how pace and beauty can go hand-in-hand with truth to a great dramatist's genius and intentions. The conflicts, and the symbol, emerged clear, vivid and dramatic, the play was far more finely acted and spoken than in any productions of recent memory, and Patrick Robertson's classically simple setting of streaked skies and pillars, lit by torchlight and with costumes glowing in contrasts of black and lime green, saffron and indigo, gave a splendid dignity, stature and atmosphere to the tragedy. Imaginative lighting did the rest, and the play moved with a leopard's grace, muscular harmony and forward spring, without geographical complications, to its tragic climax.

It would, of course, even so have foundered without a fine Lear, and Eric Porter—'a Rembrandt portrait', wrote *The Times*—rose magnificently at the performance I saw to his supreme Bristol challenge. He is an actor not always predictable in his effect, and for all the precise detail and depth of insight of his characterisations he has not always evaded a certain sombreness, a lack of *élan*, in his performances which seems to spring from some inward sadness or heaviness of mind. Here, at any rate, in a splendid and utterly convincing assumption of age and authority, he flung spiritually free and struck, like lightning on a rock, anguish and tragic fire out of the character. He rode the storm as it should be ridden—like a Blake prophet on a winged horse—but in a performance in which the intelligence never wavered in a single detail, the memorable moments were often quiet: the long passage with the Fool, for instance, after the banishment of Cordelia, when the old man winced under the lash of the Fool's tongue and showed a grief and uncertainty beyond anger—almost welcoming the images that recall a past wrong and pain. In the scene with the blind Gloucester, too, he was touching—no less than in the final agony over Cordelia's body. He was not great in madness, but touched greatness in nearly everything else. And his stillness no less than his rage could nobly command the stage.

He was helped much by Alan Dobie's brilliant Fool—bright in motley, quick in wits, professional in somersaults and repartee, but with a sting in his tongue that just prevented his being memorable—as, for instance, Alec Guinness and Stephen Haggard were memorable—in the pathos of his decline in the storm. Moira Shearer's Cordelia, too, had enough of Lear's own obstinate candour to give a suggestion of the real *conflict* of love that smoulders and finally flares out in their first scene together: a noble princess this, beautiful in her copper hair, crown and rich blue dress, with a deepening but mellow voice that could reflect the scorn of her eye as the sisters plugged their insincere compliments. Her renunciation of them and her homeland was royal; and there was a new power of projection in feeling which, though no less regal, became tenderly apparent in the reconciliation with Lear. I remember no interpretation so satisfactory in reconciling the qualities of character Cordelia inherited from her father with the gentle but passionate capacity for pity and affection that runs like a spring within the outer rock.

Phyllida Law's classically handsome Regan was rock without a spring, a fine contrast, and only Sheila Burrell's Goneril tended to weaken the forces of evil. A good actress, she was too small and delicate in build, and too low in voice, to match her sisters' effect. John Humphry, with a strong new challenging Roman nose, made a tall and striking figure of Edmund, dark and finely spoken and motivated impressively by evil, if a little missing the flash of Renaissance humour and *enjoyment* that lies within the part. Derek Godfrey's Edgar assumed persuasively the role of commentator, with a feeling for silence and a grave undercurrent of authority. And Edward Hardwicke's beautifully spoken, convincingly middle-aged and deeply moving Gloucester justified a surprising piece of casting and won generous critical praise.

The ten-year wheel was now full circle; and *King Lear* was a noble close to a decade. This book should close there, but some of the work in the new cycle cannot be overlooked. The following play, Max Frisch's *Don Juan* or *The Love of Geometry*, in a translation by Nell Moody, was a new version of the old legend that pleased some while striking others as heavy-handed. Moira Shearer strengthened her growing reputation as a lovely prostitute turned Duchess who cages Don Juan at last, and the settings and costumes of Disley Jones were praised for surpassing beauty; but after *King Lear* this was a trough in the wave, and the actors were aware of it.

Porter, an actor sculptured to the Michelangelo proportions of Lear, is not happily tuned to Don Juanism—even an intellectualised Don Juan who prefers the chaste symbols of mathematics to the ardent pursuit of women—and it proved his last performance for the company. Whatever the other factors, his physical need for rest was understandable; he had been heavily overworked in a series of long and exhausting parts and stage experience proves no actor can bear the weight of such a repertory beyond a certain point (Wreford had had a minor physical breakdown at much the same point the previous year, and had wisely been 'rested' during the production of *Image in the Sun* before tackling the role of Shylock). Porter's going was nevertheless a loss, for some of the later repertory had been planned with him in mind.

The shock was broken to a large extent by Shearer's greatest triumph, the part of Sabina in *The Skin of Our Teeth*, in which her charm was as potent as her volubility and technical prowess. Her performance should, wrote John Bennett, 'bring her an Old

169

Vic degree—with a load of honours. . . . In this Thornton Wilder play, with a voice much richer and more facile than we have ever heard from her, she gives a performance which glitters with brilliant facets. Her voice dances through it as happily as her feet once graced the ballet. It marks her real arrival as an actress—as a star'. 'Electrifying performance of prize play' was Coe's head-line, and Royston Morley's production showed that Wilder's cartoon of human existence and its powers of survival has lost nothing of its pungency, wit and tragic undercurrents with the years. It is an extravaganza whose chronological tricks all end in a contemporary thrust, and the humanities were beautifully pre-served in Eve Watkinson's Mrs. Antrobus and Derek Godfrey's incisive, ironic, moving and richly credible Mr. Antrobus—a remarkable portrait for so young an actor. Phyllida Law's buxom gypsy fortune-teller was also a striking metamorphosis, and Alan Dobie's Henry had all the marks of the original crazy mixed-up kid, Cain. The play dazzled and deeply moved: the Bristol Old Vic was itself again.

Another fine play followed on April 17th, Peter Ustinov's *The Empty Chair*, an Anatomy of Revolution he had written specially for the company. This magnificent play, literary in style but dramatic in its implications and theme, has still not (in January 1957) been seen in London, but more serious in tone, more sharply ironic in wit and political comment than his other recent plays, it shows a mind of a new maturity and power with a grasp not only of the conflicting characters behind an insurrection, but the flaws in the structure of a State, ballasted by abuse of power, which send revolution, even successful revolution, spinning in reverse as the great men founder. The empty throne in which, one by one, the doomed men—Hébert, Danton, Robespierre—sit is a symbol of destruction but also of the new eras that rise from it. We are left (after slightly too long a last act) with the smaller man, Barras, evading its death-clutches and the shadow of Napoleon and the new Empire looming as the banner of revolution falls.

Alan Dobie was a coldly vivid Robespierre, the incorruptible with a flaw, Joseph O'Conor, Porter's successor, a perhaps over-rough but vigorous Danton, and Derek Godfrey as an apocryphal and very Ustinovian 'spy with a soul' called Mouche slid insinu-ating out of cupboards to make a dry comment on the lack of disinterest in politics. John Humphry, too, gave a notable insolence to Barras, and Moira Shearer played sensitively the small part of a Charwoman—one of the three acting as chorus to the play. Moody's production, however, tended to be static and lacked the cumulative drama and sword-thrusts of climax achieved later by Frank Dunlop in an Arts Council touring production.

In *The Rivals* Humphry in the difficult role of Faulkland incontestably carried off the palm, both in Bristol and at the Zürich Festival, where the play was given by the Old Vic Company by request. 'A superbly polished nonentity whose anaemic attempts at love are a joy to watch', wrote Bushell. 'Here is perfect repose and control—rare gifts on the stage today.' *The Stage* was equally emphatic: 'Where this production immediately excels is in John Humphry's Faulkland, a superb portrayal of extreme sensibility. With delicately fluttering hands, a constantly exaggerated posture and cast from ecstasy to deepest melancholy in a moment, Mr. Humphry plays with rare flourish.' And *The Times* on the Zürich production considered 'This revival of the cheerful old comedy is as good an example of repertory teamwork as comes to mind, and the Bristol company is particularly fortunate to have at the moment an actor of the talent of Mr. John Humphry to play Faulkland, which is quite the most difficult part in the play. It may not be quite true to say that a production of *The Rivals* stands or falls by Faulkland, but a good interpretation of this character can give the play a quality it might not otherwise possess. In this instance there is further cause for satisfaction, for Mr. Joseph O'Conor's Sir Antony Absolute is a reading full of amusing irascibility and comic business. Mr. Alan Dobie's cheerful Bob Acres, Miss Moira Shearer's ineffably romantic Lydia Languish, and Miss Eve Watkinson's Mrs. Malaprop, whose malapropisms fairly rattled across the stage, lent the play just the right air of festival. Since *The Rivals* was played at the Theatre Royal, Bristol, in May the production has been speeded up and polished. It now shines brightly. . . .'

A strange modern play followed on May 29th, *The Castle of Deception*, a 'bogus verse' play by Peter Philp, which had already attracted attention in repertory and on the Third Programme of the B.B.C. Its theme of the comparative values of the bogus and the real centres on a rich eccentric's house with its collection of fake antiques, supplemented by a fake 'Russian' count, a fake painter of classical masterpieces, and a fake prostitute who loves the painter. In a brilliant setting by Disley Jones it held one's fascinated interest, but tended to dissipate its opening sinister and expressionistic effect with a more novelettish romance and dialogue later. It was a play that, though absorbing and intelligent up to a point, moved on too many levels for success, but its superb central part is a challenge to a character actor of genius, and Porter had influenced the choice of the play. O'Conor played the eccentric cleverly but with a touch of grotesque caricature it does not really demand, and the climax of his madness therefore lacked poignancy and power. Humphry was the Count, Shearer the blameless 'tart', Phyllida Law the wife and Dobie the painter. Warren Jenkins admirably produced.

Major Barbara, the final play, was chosen as a Shaw tribute in the dramatist's centenary year and moved after the Bristol run to the London Old Vic in July. It was not Moira Shearer's ideal and greatest part, though she played it with charm, intelligence and some force of emotion in the second act. Joseph O'Conor's Undershaft was a stronger part and performance, very incisively characterised and played, if not quite of the stature of the Old Vic's last Undershaft, the late (and incomparable) Cecil Trouncer. And Derek Godfrey was the perfect Cusins, his Greek Professor banging a Salvation Army drum with a diabolic gleam of irony behind scholarly rimless spectacles, but catching the note of charm and tender indulgence in the relationship with Barbara. Alan Dobie as Bill Walker, Edward Hardwicke as 'Snobby' Price and Peter O'Toole as the respectable ageing workman Peter were also outstandingly in character in the Salvation Army setting, a superb piece of work by Patrick Robertson in the cinematic tradition with the French slum. Otherwise the company was not truly at its best, rather immature and slow to measure up to the acoustics of the Waterloo Road theatre.

Thus ended the tenth anniversary season: rightly in the London Old Vic, the parent home. The work is not ended, however, but continuous, and with Rachel Roberts, Alan Dobie and Joseph O'Conor heading the company, thrusts into 1957 with a new barrage of plays, from Bristol's first Ugo Betti play, *The Queen and the Rebels*, to *Othello* and *Pygmalion*. The future may and must hold changes of directorship and actors, but the essential pattern is preserved; the interchange of artists between the London and

Bristol Old Vic continues; and both organisations can only benefit from this circulation of the theatre's life-blood. It is for the actors, producers and dramatists of the future to meet the challenge, and preserve something that has brought a new vigour into the English provincial theatre, and built up already many players of future eminence. [A.W.]

AN OCCASIONAL PROLOGUE TO
SHE STOOPS TO CONQUER

Written by Herbert Farjeon and spoken by Dame Sybil Thorndike in the character of Mrs. Hardcastle at the reopening of the Theatre Royal, Bristol, May 11th, 1943.

So! there you sit once more!—pit, circle, boxes;
Sparks, matrons, coxcombs, critics with their doxies,
Assembl'd as of old; spry, spruce, expecting;
Some looking forward; others recollecting;
All brisk, all bubbling, British and Bristolian
As in the days of Nelson and Napoleon
When, on this stage, Hamlets were lit by tapers;
And press-gangs weren't confin'd to daily papers;
When Desdemonas, chok'd in tragic error,
Made refugees forget the Reign of Terror;
And the Prince Regent—I can still see him—sat in
That very box, he used to look so fat in.
Yes, there again you are, fresh from your coaches,
Prepar'd with praises, ready with reproaches,
Back at your old game of adjudication,
Agog to make or mar a reputation—
I don't care which it is, I'm so delighted!
Who ever thought we should be reunited?
A narrow squeak, I vow! but worth the trouble,
For hang it! ha'n't we had our fill of rubble?
Treasures like this—if we should slight or spurn 'em,
Can we condemn the foe who'd bomb and burn 'em?
So when Sir Kingsley told us that for staving
Defeat, there was no saving grace like saving,
We took him at his word, and, strictly loyal,
For England's honour, sav'd—the Theatre Royal.
Nay, we did more; with one eye on production,
We boldly led the way in reconstruction,
Till, of our oldest theatre, 'twould be truest
To say, it's both our oldest and our newest.
Here, then, it stands; unique and unpretentious;
Lawfully licensed, and yet not licentious;

Coy but inviting; chaste but full of feeling;
Unscath'd from floor to star-encrusted ceiling—
O stars! O actors who, in days gone by,
Trod where we tread, now, in mimic sky
Enspher'd, shine down with tutelary grace
On us who humbly strive to fill your place:
Great Siddons, once, majestic and aloof,
Queen of these boards, now regal in the roof;
Old Kean, whose Richard froze the breath of laughter,
Now kindling your successors from the rafter;
Garrick, who once was king and now is loam,
Still twinkling bright, a spangle in the dome;
Kemble, Macready, Macklin, Foote—Lord love you,
And Lord love them! they are all up there above you,
Cut out in little stars; and one so shining,
One so responsive to the heart's inclining,
So generous, so sweet, so fair, so merry,
That all beholders know it for Ellen Terry.
Well, Ellen! David! Sarah! here and now
We register and consecrate a vow,
As worthily as in our power lies
To earn your smiles and not provoke your sighs;
To honour and to keep the faith unbroken
That may be felt but never can be spoken;
To carry on the work that you began;
Even to rouse your envy if we can;
Making it our endeavour, first and last,
To serve the present and deserve the past.
But Comedy calls!—I mustn't be too serious—
Comedy, classic, clear, and unmysterious,
Stooping to conquer, curtseying to slay,
Restive behind here to get under way,
Champing the bit and chafing to do battle—
On with the ponies, then, and cut the prattle!
And should their prancing fail, alas! to please you,
Remember still—since prologues should appease you—
That, as in love and war initial ardour
Is easy, but to keep it up is harder,
The favour you bestow on us in starting
Will be twice welcome if bestow'd when parting.

HERBERT FARJEON

(This prologue was specially commissioned by C.E.M.A. and is published by permission of Mrs. Herbert Farjeon and the Arts Council of Great Britain.)

PROLOGUE

OPENING PRODUCTION OF THE BRISTOL OLD VIC

Written by Christopher Hassall for the performance of
The Beaux' Stratagem. *Spoken in the character of Will*
Boniface by Mr. Robert Sansom, February 19th, 1946.

Pardon me, gentles, butting in like this.
All's well behind the curtain. Naught's amiss
—Except the Prologue, as the saying is.
Od's life, my lords, I'm not inured to rhyme
Or mixing poetry and petty crime.
A gentleman may count on Boniface
To roast a capon, keep his proper place,
Or make amends for speaking out of turn,
But prologues cost me blood and tears to learn.
I'm landlord here, in our ensuing scene,
Vexed out of mind as never man has been.
Witness yourselves anon my load of worry,
See me distracted, hear the hurry-scurry
Of bells at jingle-jangle, knockers rapping
Dogs broken loose and wanting bones and yapping,
And surly grooms, awash with liquor, scrapping
Among the trunks they ought to be unstrapping.
—The coach from Warrington has caught us napping!
And still my daughter, heedless of the din,
Delays, od's tooth, to let the travellers in.
What else, sir, would a father pay her for
But looking dainty as she opes the door?
'Tis I keeps watch a-nights and drinks my fill,
Fetches the warming-pans, or at the till
Juggles the change when gentry pay the bill.
    Tonight's the night, my lords, and this the place,
Or split me windpipe, I'm not Boniface!
Small wonder modern folk still marvel at a gem
Of high adventure such as our Beaux' Stratagem.
Here's back-stage cunning, daggers, cloaks, disguises,
The rich and handsome getting all the prizes,

Rope-ladders, robberies at point of pistol,
And other ruderies unknown to Bristol.
In sooth, we'll play some old-world saucy tricks
Will make you glad of Nineteen-forty-six.
But hold—it ain't our purpose every week
To wear the buckle-shoe and talk antique.
We'll race the calendar with comedies
Hot from the oven, as the saying is,
Or plays whose problems somewhat in the dark are,
—A far cry, as the saying is, from Farquhar.
But old or new, we're sworn to bring the best,
As well befits the Old Vic of the West.
By your good leave, we're yours—not passing through,
As certain of our friends are wont to do,
En route, they hope, for Shaftesbury Avenue—
But yours to applaud, or censure if we fail;
Yours either way, says I, to drink your ale.
Must London, with St. Paul's and all the soot,
Have all the Drama's cakes and ale to boot?
The Arts, confined to no especial place,
Follow the questing spirit of the race. . . .
Od's breath, I couldn't talk so had I slipt
One syllable from the appointed script
Penn'd in a fervour and expressly sent
To spice the welcome of the management!
But I forget! The coach from Warrington!
Now where's my daughter? Sirs, I must be gone.
There's custom waiting. Gentle folks, be merry.
All's topsy-turvy. (As he goes) Cherry! . . . daughter . . . Cherry!

CHRISTOPHER HASSALL

PROLOGUE

TENTH ANNIVERSARY OF THE BRISTOL OLD VIC

*Written by Christopher Hassall. Spoken by Yvonne
Mitchell, February 18th, 1956.*

Ten years, and still afloat? What prodigy
What more than nine days' wonder can this be?
Not only solvent still—but *popular*
Not even transformed into a cinema?
This proves the living Theatre cannot die.
The Muses are amazed, and so am I.
  Beaux' Stratagem was our inaugural play.
The Prologue then is valid still today;
Its verses mark'd our point of origin,
Though spoken by the Landlord of an Inn
With accent oafish. How did he begin?
The tabs were closed. He entered, left, I think.
'Tonight's the night,' he cried, 'and this the place,
Or split me windpipe, I'm not Boniface!'
—More followed, then he tumbled from the brink—
' 'Tis not', said he, 'our purpose every week
To wear the buckle-shoe and talk antique.
We'll race the calendar with comedies
Hot from the oven, as the saying is,
Or plays whose problems somewhat in the dark are
—A far cry, as the saying is, from Farquhar.
But old or new, we're sworn to bring the best
As well befits the Old Vic of the West.
By your good leave, we're yours—not passing through
As certain of our friends are wont to do,
En route, they hope, for Shaftesbury Avenue—
But yours to applaud, or censure if we fail;
Yours either way, say I, to drink your ale.
Must London, with St. Paul's and all the soot,
Have all the Drama's cakes and ale to boot?

The Arts, confined to no especial place,
Follow the questing spirit of the race. . . .'
  Such was the drift of old Will Boniface
Ten years ago (when I, your servant, played
The spry role of a Restoration maid).
Such our first prologue, yet the selfsame bard,
Told of this gala evening, found it hard
To rhyme. Astonished, he could hardly speak.
(I think he must have thought we'd last a week.)
Chewing his pencil, he at last turned broody.
Who wouldn't, faced with a span from Hunt to Moody
With Carey in between? He rubb'd his eyes
And read a tale of tireless enterprise—
Fry, Eliot, and many a modern more,
Of Shakespeare plays the total now a score,
Pantos, experiments and even plays
Born on the spot! What else is *Salad Days?*
—That home-grown dish exported far from home
To show the shape of musicals to come!
And stars have risen here. To name a few
Take Neville, Tutin, Rogers, Sellars too.
The Muse of Drama, flushed with her success
Has made this house her permanent address,
Proud to frequent this legendary stage,
To prosper and deserve your patronage.
We are at once her servants, friends, and yours
Who queue up staunchly at the early doors.
Bless our new venture as you bless'd the last
And we'll not prove unworthy of the past,
But strive afresh, by virtue of your aid,
To win your applause throughout the next decade.

CHRISTOPHER HASSALL

THE BRISTOL OLD VIC THEATRE SCHOOL

Winners of the Annual Award made by the Bristol Evening
Post *to the most promising first year student.*

1951   Phyllida Law.

1952   John Milligan.

1953   Barbara Leigh-Hunt.

1954   Annette Crosbie.

1955   Bernard Behrens.

1956   Valerie Gearon.

Index of Persons and Organisations

Index of Plays